Spotlight On

Madrid

Harvey Holtom

Written by Harvey Holtom

Published by AA Publishing, a trading name of Automobile Association Developments Limited, whose registered office is Fanum House, Basing View, Basingstoke, Hampshire, RG21 4EA. Registered number 1878835.

Packaged for Automobile Association Developments Limited by IL&FS, New Delhi

A CIP catalogue record for this book is available from the British Library.

ISBN 978-0-7495-5783-6

The contents of this publication are believed correct at the time of printing. Nevertheless, the publishers cannot be held responsible for any errors or omissions or for changes in the details given in this guide or for the consequences of any reliance on the information provided by the same. Assessments of attractions, hotels, restaurants and so forth are based on the author's own experience and, therefore, descriptions given in this guide necessarily contain an element of subjective opinion which may not reflect the publishers' opinion or dictate a reader's own experience on another occasion. We have tried to ensure accuracy in this guide, but things do change and we would be grateful if readers would advise us of any inaccuracies they may encounter.

Colour separation by KDP
Printed and bound in China by Leo Paper Products

914.60483
HOL

A03697
Maps in this title produced from maps © MAIRDUMONT / Falk Verlag 2008
Transport map © Communicarta Ltd, UK

REYNANDO
CARLOSIICOB
ERNANDODO
ÑAMARYANA
SVMADRE16I4

CONTENTS

Palacio and the West

Centro

Jerónimos and the East

Chueca and the North

Further Afield

Listings

Madrid

Like all great capitals, Madrid has extremely humble origins. Unlike most other great capitals, Madrid was perhaps never really destined to become the vibrant metropolis it is today. Or maybe not even a capital at all. Most other European capitals sit astride mighty rivers; landlocked Madrid offers only the oft-ridiculed Manzanares, a large stream at best. Some were always strategic hubs, being located on trade routes or close to natural resources; not so Madrid.

Many were important centres in Roman times; Madrid, apart from a few small settlements nearby, has no Roman past to speak of, much less a glorious one. More to the point, for a country which had been forged in the struggle to oust the Moors who dominated much of the Iberian Peninsula for around seven centuries, Madrid has the irksome inconvenience of having been founded, around 860 BC, by that very enemy.

Yet somehow this medium-sized but totally insignificant town, home to scarcely 20,000 souls, became almost overnight the capital of an immense seaborne empire. One might reasonably ask – how?

Madrid owes its capital city status to the decision of one man, King Philip II. On 11 May, 1561, Philip sent out a letter to the minor aristocrats of the "*villa de Madrid*" – *villa* means "town", city status was still far in the future. It informed them that he, the royal household and the entire travelling court – who numbered hundreds – would be visiting this town and could they please prepare to receive their illustrious callers. While this move caused panic amongst the hosts – feeding and accommodating all these guests posed a major problem – what they did not know was that Philip planned to establish the capital here permanently, an unprecedented move, as the court had long been itinerant. The idea was not so mad. Philip took his kingly duties very seriously, and running his enormous, unwieldy empire with an itinerant court was impractical. A permanent seat was called for.

But why Madrid? For this was a town with no cathedral, no university and no printing press, and with only that apology for a river! Hardly anyone's first choice. In the 1540s, though, Philip – while still the crown prince – had already commissioned the conversion of Madrid's Alcázar, the former Arab fortress, into a sizeable palace. Evidently, his idea, though whimsical, was premeditated. Possibly the town's location bang in the centre of the peninsula appealed to his geometric mind. He may have shied away from Toledo and Valladolid, because they had too much historical baggage, rivalry and agendas of their own. Philip wanted a purpose-built capital, one to suit his designs. The die was thus cast – Madrid was plucked from obscurity to play a leading role on a huge stage.

This hurried and improvised transformation brought vertiginous and chaotic growth over the following decades. In that time, all manner of fortune seekers and *pícaros*, undesirables, converged on Madrid in the hope of making a quick buck, or *real* as the Spanish coin was called. It quickly became a town of outsiders, something it still is today. Habsburg Madrid compared most unfavourably with its European counterparts. Apart from a few major projects – such as the Plaza Mayor, extensions to the city walls and lots of churches and monasteries – it had few embellishments of note.

Much would change in the 18th and 19th centuries, with the Bourbon dynasty. Grand urban projects were carried out, the Paseo

del Prado was created, monasteries were disentailed and replaced by elegant squares, the Palacio Real replaced the burnt-down Alcázar, the Prado Museum was built, and monuments were erected. Curiously, though, until the last third of the 19th century, Madrid remained confined within its old city walls. It was only after the 1860 expansion plan was approved that the modern city began to take shape. Even then, it would not be until the later 20th century that Madrid could unselfconsciously feel it was able to rub shoulders with the best.

Now it can. Madrid has stopped contemplating its own navel and wondering what its role in the world is. It is now confident, dynamic and forward-looking, less parochial and more open. Inserted into the globalised world, Madrid has recently welcomed an influx of newcomers once again – now from further afield than ever before.

People visit Madrid nowadays for many different reasons. How you spend your time here depends on what you like. And you can do whatever you like. If eating and drinking is your thing, Madrid rarely disappoints. The traditional and excellent Spanish food that has always been on offer is now complemented by an ever-growing range of more exotic fare. In-the-know nighthawks know Madrid is a city that never sleeps, and will find action into the wee hours.

If you want culture, you have it by the lorry-load. Museum-goers have the Golden Triangle – the Prado, the Thyssen and the Reina Sofía are three of the world's greatest art palaces. It doesn't stop there, though, for the many lesser museums and private foundations will keep you busy for days, and throughout the year there are events such as the ARCO, PhotoEspaña or Estampa. If the performing arts are your bag, regular programmes plus seasonal festivals such as the January Flamenco Festival, the spring-time Madrid en Danza, the summer Veranos de la Villa and the autumn Festival de Otoño will quench your thirst. Inveterate sightseers may find Madrid less monumental than Rome or Paris, but will take delight in the Plaza Mayor, the Puerta de Alcalá, the imposing Palacio Real or the many splendid churches and monasteries dotted around the old city.

Shopaholics nowadays find Madrid anything but the consumer backwater it used to be. From the hip Fuencarral market to the elegant designer stores of Barrio Salamanca, without forgetting the Rastro flea market on Sundays, you can splash that cash with gay abandon. Fans of the beautiful game can choose between Real Madrid's grandiose Bernabéu stadium and Atlético de Madrid's humbler, but passionate Calderón.

Street parties are a local speciality. Be here for the carnival, the 2 May festivities, San Isidro two weeks later, or the August *verbenas* (religious fairs and celebrations) in the old city. Then you will see Madrileños doing what they love doing, and what they do best: having fun. Because having fun, when all is said and done, is what this city is about.

MONCLOA

CIUDAD
UNIVERSITARIA

VALLEHERMOSO

Sala de Exposiciones
del Canal de Isabel II

CHAMBERÍ

Museo
del Traje

Museo de
América

ARAPILES

GAZTÁMBIDE

TRAFALGAR

Parque
del Oeste

PALACIO
& THE WEST
14-57

ARGÜELLES

UNIVERSIDAD

Plaza
dos de Mayo

Ermita de
San Antonio
de la Florida

Casa de
Campo

Río Manzanares

Museo
Cerralbo

Plaza de
España

Estación de
Príncipe Pío

Monasterio de
la Encarnación

Calle Gran Vía

Lago Casa
de Campo

Palacio
Real

Plaza de
Oriente

Monasterio
de las Descalzas
Reales

SOL

Real Academia
de Bellas Artes
de San Fernando

Convento de
las Carboneras

PALACIO

Calle
Arenal

San Nicolás
de los Servitas

Calle
Mayor

Puerta
del Sol

Catedral
de la Almudena

Plaza de
la Villa

Plaza
Mayor

Muralla
Árabe

Arco de los
Cuchilleros

Plaza de
Santa Ana

El Viaducto

Plaza del Conde
de Barajas

Basílica de
San Miguel

CENTRO

Jardines de
las Vistillas

San Pedro
el Viejo

Plaza de
la Paja

Colegiata de
San Isidro

CENTRO
58-99

Basílica de
San Francisco
el Grande

Plaza de
la Cebada

Plaza de
Cascorro

Calle del
Mesón de Paredes

El Rastro

PUERTA DEL
ANGEL

EMBAJADORES

IMPERIAL

10

GUIDE TO BOOK REGIONS

0 ____ 500 m
0 ____ 500 yds

CUATRO
CAMINOS

EL
VISO

Museo de
la Ciudad

PROSPERIDAD

Botero
Sculptures

RÍOS ROSAS

Museo Lázaro
Galdiano

Museo
Sorolla

ALMAGRO

GUINDALERA

**CHUECA
& THE NORTH
124-145**

Museo de
Escultura al
Aire Libre

CASTELLANA

Fundación
Juan March

LISTA

Paseo de la
Castellana

SALAMANCA

Museo
Romántico

JUSTICIA

RECOLETOS

GOYA

Iglesia de
San Antón

Plaza
de Colón

Jardínes del
Descubrimiento

FUENTE
DEL BERRO

Santa Bárbara
(Las Salesas Reales)

Museo
Arqueológico
Nacional

Casa de las
Siete Chimeneas

Casa de
America

Puerta
de Alcalá

IBIZA

Iglesia de las
Calatravas

Plaza
de la Cibeles

Museo
Thyssen-
Bornemisza

Museo
Naval

Museo Nacional
de Artes Decorativas

CORTES

Plaza de
la Lealtad

RETIRO

Plaza de
las Cortes

Casón del
Buen Retiro

Casa Museo
Lope de Vega

San Jerónimo
El Real

NIÑO JESÚS

ESTRELLA

Museo
del Prado

JERÓNIMOS

Parque
del Retiro

**JERÓNIMOS
& THE EAST
100-123**

Jardín
Botánico

Museo Nacional
Reina Sofía

PACÍFICO

Estación
de Atocha

Real Fábrica
de Tapices

Palacio and the West

A cursory glance at the map of this area reveals a lot of green, meaning that any time spent exploring it will inevitably include gorgeous leafy parks, which is very pleasant. But this area also includes the spot where it all began, when the Moors established their garrison town Magerit, in the area occupied nowadays by the Palacio Real and Plaza de Oriente. Wandering around here shows you that royal core as well as offering you some stunning views to the west. It also takes you to some fascinating churches, museums with engaging collections, and several impressive open squares.

PALACIO AND THE WEST WALK

1. Basilica de San Francisco el Grande
See page 18

Exit from La Latina metro station (on line 5) to Plaza de la Cebada. Walk past the Cebada market and carry on into the extension of this street, which is the Carrera de San Francisco. Stop halfway down and admire the impressive neo-classical façade of the Basilica. Then head north up the Calle de Bailén.

2. Plaza de Oriente See page 52

Going north along Calle de Bailén, enjoy the views over the Casa de Campo from the viaduct. Carry on past the Catedral de la Almudena, and then take in the majestic sweep of the Plaza de Oriente. Enjoy a coffee in the elegant Café de Oriente, meander through the gardens and admire the façade of the Palacio Real, the statues of Spanish kings and the rear view of the Teatro Real, Madrid's opera house.

3. Plaza de España See page 50

Leaving Plaza de Oriente through the northwest corner, continue along Bailén towards the Plaza de España over the road bridge. In the centre of the square, the statue of writer Miguel de Cervantes serenely observes two of his literary creations, Don Quixote and his sidekick Sancho Panza. The 25-floor Edificio España and the 36-storey Torre de Madrid dominate the northeast corner of the square.

4. Parque del Oeste See page 48

Exit Plaza de España via the northwest corner and cross Calle de Ferraz. Up the little hill is the 2nd-century Egyptian Templo de Debod, donated by Egypt in 1968 in return for Spain's help in saving monuments during the buidling of the Aswan Dam. Wander north on the Paseo del Pintor Rosales. Enter the park, meander around, go south to the Rosaleda gardens, then head down Calle Francisco y Jacinto Alcántara, leaving the park towards the railway lines.

5. Ermita de San Antonio de la Florida
See page 24

Leave the Parque del Oeste, crossing over the pedestrian footbridge. You will come out just a few metres north of the Glorieta de San Antonio de la Florida. Here you will find a charming little neo-classical hermitage dedicated to St Anthony of Padua, which has frescoes by Goya as well as the great painter's own tomb.

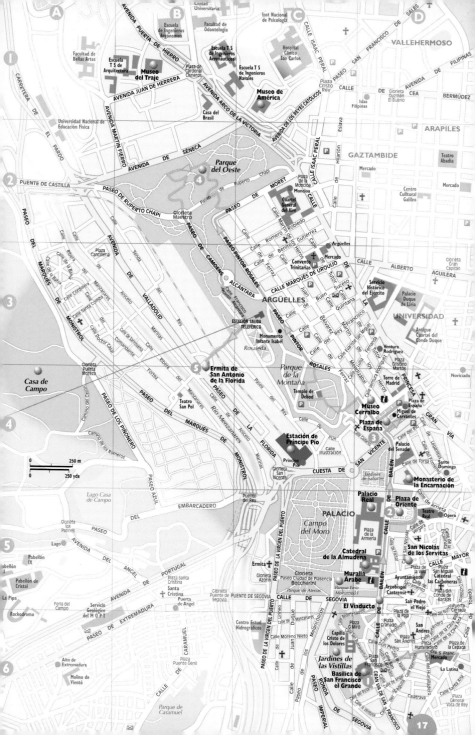

Basilica de San Francisco

This is one of Madrid's largest churches and, when approaching from La Latina down the Carrera de San Francisco, is impossible to miss. It occupies a site where there was once a Franciscan monastery founded, legend has it, by St Francis of Assisi in 1217. In 1760, King Carlos III ordered the demolition of the monastery and its replacement with a church. The result was this splendid neo-classical edifice, built between 1761 and 1784.

Work was initiated by Francisco Cabezas; but in 1774, the Italian architect Francesco Sabatini assumed control of the project and completed it.

✚ **17 D6**

✉ **Basilica de San Francisco**
Plaza de San Francisco

☎ 91 365 3800

◷ Sep–Jul Tue–Fri 11–12:30 (also Sat if no church services being held) and 4–6:30; Aug Tue–Sun 11–12:30 and 5–7:30

♿ Inexpensive (guided tours only)

Ⓜ La Latina or Puerta de Toledo (line 5)

In 1836, under the act of disendowment of church properties carried out by the minister Mendizábal, the basilica was expropriated and used as an army barracks until 1869. Later it was converted into the national pantheon.

Then in 1878, the Spanish council of ministers proposed that it become a national church – as at that time Madrid had no cathedral – for state ceremonies and it thus underwent extensive restoration work. The Franciscan order renovated the basilica in 1926 and it was consecrated anew in 1962. Once again, from the mid-1970s until 2001, it was subject to further restoration work.

The basilica, with Sabatini's marvellous neo-classical façade, is dominated by its huge dome, which measures 33m (108 feet) in diameter, making it larger than St Paul's in London and one of the largest in the world. Now restored, the inside of the dome is covered by an ambitious series of religious paintings by Carlos Luis de Rivera. The seven chapels that surround the main rotunda contain a huge collection of outstanding paintings. There are works by Goya, Zurbarán, Alonso Cano, Maella and Casado del Alisal, along with marble sculptures by Ricardo Bellver and Mariano Benlliure. Also to be admired are the beautiful stained-glass windows, which were made by the German firm Mayer.

Above: The imposing Basilica de San Francisco

Casa de Campo

Occupying some 1,820ha (almost 4,500 acres), the Casa de Campo is the largest public park in Europe. The land was formerly a royal hunting ground and was only opened to the public in 1931.

Situated to the west of central Madrid, the Casa de Campo is not far and is easily accessible by bus, metro and cable car – the Teleférico, as this last is called, leaves from the Parque del Oeste (see page 48) and is possibly the most enjoyable way of getting there.

During the Spanish Civil War (1936–9), when republican Madrid was besieged by Franco's nationalist forces, the city centre and the university were shelled from the higher slopes of the park, and to this day, it is possible to see remains of the trenches that were dug here.

Nowadays the Casa de Campo is given over to more peaceful leisure pursuits, and for thousands of Madrileños it is a place to relax, have fun, get some fresh air, enjoy a picnic and take part in many outdoor activities, mountain biking being a popular one.

There certainly are many attractions. One of the best-loved spots is the large boating lake with a geyser spouting water in the centre. The many cafés dotted around its edges are hugely popular in good weather. Near by are the swimming pools, close to Lago metro station. A short distance away is the Recinto Ferial of the Casa de Campo, an exhibition and congress centre that includes the Telefónica Arena, a multi-purpose venue which hosts concerts, basketball matches and, since 2002, the prestigious Madrid Masters tennis tournament.

Not far away is the Parque de Atracciones, a permanent funfair, with many rides, some quite hair-raising, for all ages and tastes. A little deeper into the park is Madrid's zoo, which boasts an impressive aquarium in which sharks glide around menacingly and are a fascinating draw to children and adults.

Left: Flamingos in the zoo at Casa de Campo

🕀 **17 A4**

✉ **Casa de Campo**
Casa de Campo

🚇 Lago or Batán

Catedral de la Almudena

The city's Catholic cathedral, the Catedral de Santa María la Real de la Almudena – to give it its full title – is not the most stunning of buildings. But it has a long and interesting history that reflects that of Madrid itself.

The site next to the Palacio Real originally housed the city's main mosque and was reconsecrated in the 11th century, when the city was taken back from the Moors by the Spaniards and a church was built, dedicated to the Virgin Mary.

As the city grew, so did discussion between state and church about whether it should have its own cathedral – something hotly disputed by rival city Toledo. Only one thing was certain, and that was that any cathedral would be dedicated to Madrid's female patron saint, the Virgin de

Left: The façade of Catedral de la Almudena; **above:** The cathedral at dusk

✚ **17 D5**

✉ **Catedral de la Almudena**
Calle de Bailén 10

☎ 91 542 2200, museum 91 559 2874

🕐 Sep–Jun daily 10–2, 5–8; Jul–Aug 10–2, 5–9; museum Mon–Sat 10–2:30, closed Sun

🎫 Cathedral free, museum moderate (guided tour only)

🚇 Ópera

la Almudena. According to one legend, an image of the Virgin was hidden in the city walls to keep it from the invading Muslim force. Some say her name derives from the Arabic *al-mudayna*, which means "citadel" or "city".

It wasn't until 1885, when Pope Leon XIII ordered the creation of the diocese of Madrid-Alcalá, that the city was allowed to posses its own cathedral. However, it was to take a further 110 years to complete. First to have a go in 1883 was the architect Francisco, Marqués de Cubas, who began with the dream of recreating the Gothic splendour of a church of the Middle Ages, laid out in the form of a Latin cross. But lack of money and an overambitious design meant building ground to a halt after only the crypt (access from Calle Mayor) had been built.

Work continued but stopped again altogether during the Civil War. In the 1940s, it was decided the Gothic design would clash with the neo-classical style of the cathedral's grand neighbour, the Palacio Real, and plans were altered to bring the two into line. In the 1950s, architect Fernando Chueca Goitia took up the reins – only to have the project falter again due to financial constraints!

Work continued until 1999, but the cathedral was declared complete in 1993 in order that Pope John Paul II, making his fourth visit to Spain, might consecrate it. Almudena is the first Spanish cathedral consecrated by a pope – indeed it is the first cathedral that a pope has consecrated outside Rome.

The 102m (335-feet) long, 73m (240-feet) high building is imposing from outside but

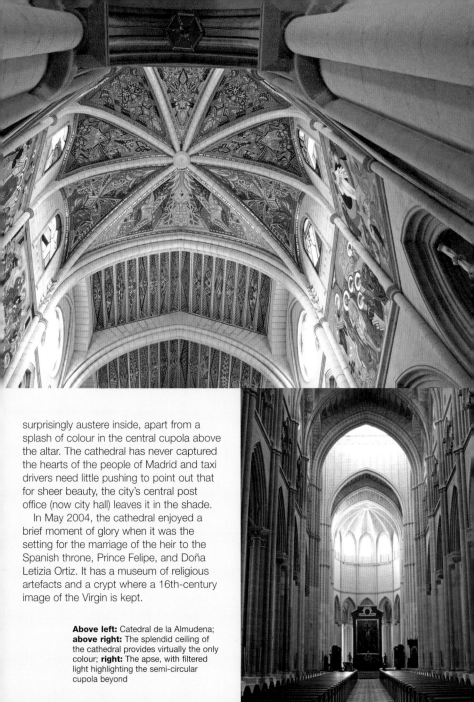

surprisingly austere inside, apart from a splash of colour in the central cupola above the altar. The cathedral has never captured the hearts of the people of Madrid and taxi drivers need little pushing to point out that for sheer beauty, the city's central post office (now city hall) leaves it in the shade.

In May 2004, the cathedral enjoyed a brief moment of glory when it was the setting for the marriage of the heir to the Spanish throne, Prince Felipe, and Doña Letizia Ortiz. It has a museum of religious artefacts and a crypt where a 16th-century image of the Virgin is kept.

Above left: Catedral de la Almudena; **above right:** The splendid ceiling of the cathedral provides virtually the only colour; **right:** The apse, with filtered light highlighting the semi-circular cupola beyond

Ermita de San Antonio de la Florida

A little off the beaten track, but actually only a short walk from Príncipe Pío station, stands the Real Ermita (royal hermitage) of San Antonio de la Florida. This sober, simple little temple is considered a neo-classical jewel and is worth the visit. It was commissioned by Charles IV in response to the growing cult of San Antonio de Padua (St Anthony) and was built between 1792 and 1798 by the little-known architect Francisco Fontana on the site where two hermitages had previously stood.

As it neared completion, to mark the temple's consecration, the king commissioned Francisco de Goya to paint the frescoes that adorn the walls, cupola and ceiling. Counted among Goya's masterpieces, the frescoes are the main attraction of the temple and are the real reward for making the trek there. Goya spent four months on this project, travelling daily from his home in Madrid in a carriage specially provided for him.

The most spectacular of the frescoes is the one in the dome, which is a representation of the miracle of St Anthony, who (legend has it) was transported by angels from Padua to his native Lisbon after a devotee prayed for his help. There he raised a murder victim from the dead, who was then able to identify his murderer, thus saving St Anthony's own father, who had been wrongly accused of the crime.

A second composition – covering the pendentive, walls and the half-cupola of the high altar – portrays a group of angels and the symbol of the Holy Trinity. The principal scene shows the onlookers who witness the miracle. Goya set this scene in contemporary Madrid, with the onlookers dressed in the street attire usual at the time, thus giving it a more secular, everyday air. Against a background of blue skies, clouds and trees, we see children play, women talk and people gesticulate with an

Left: The façade of the Ermita de San Antonio de la Florida, housing a museum dedicated to the artist Goya, whose remains are buried in front of the altar

✚ **17 B4**

✉ **Ermita de San Antonio de la Florida**
Glorieta de San Antonio de la Florida 5

☎ 91 542 0722

🌐 **www.munimadrid.es/ermita**

🕐 Tue–Fri 9:30–8 (till 2:30 Aug), Sat–Sun 10–2, closed Mon and public holidays

✋ Free

🚇 Príncipe Pío (lines 6, 10 and R)

air of awe and devotion. The frescoes have been cleaned up and restored in recent times, and so can now be appreciated in their full magnificence.

Apart from the frescoes, the other main attraction of the hermitage is that it is Goya's final resting place. Initially buried in Bordeaux, the painter's remains were moved here in 1919 and the tomb is immediately visible on entering.

Just across the road that leads into the park behind the temple is another, almost identical chapel built in the 1920s, so that the original could serve solely as a museum. Here, a tradition has grown up to mark the saint's day on 13 June, in which seamstresses demand that unmarried girls must throw 13 pins into the font and then plunge their hands inside. The number of pins that stick to their hands indicates the number of suitors they will have in the coming year.

The surrounding neighbourhood, though actually little more than a stone's throw from the city centre, feels somewhat detached and certainly is not Madrid's best-trodden. Except, that is, for the hordes who are usually headed for another Madrid landmark just a few steps away. This is the Casa Mingo, an Asturian restaurant and *sidrería* (cider house) which will probably seem rather appealing after the walk to the hermitage. And for those who wish to take a stroll after their meal, there is the nearby Parque de la Bombilla, or the Manzanares river-bank – but do not expect too much, this is not the Thames!

Right: Detail from one of the many beautiful frescoes at Ermita de San Antonio de la Florida

Estación de Príncipe Pío

Originally named the Estación del Norte (North Station), Príncipe Pío was built by the grandly named Compañia de los Caminos de Hierro del Norte de España (or Railway Company of the North of Spain) in fits and starts from 1876 – when the project was first approved – to 1928.

In 1928, the façade that looks towards the Cuesta de San Vicente was finished. Two other buildings, one for passengers and the other for goods, had already been erected earlier.

Since that time, it has been bombed, rebuilt, allowed to fall into dereliction, and then rebuilt again. Nowadays it is a commuter hub for Madrid's western suburbs and dormitory towns, while three metro lines provide links to other parts of town. One moment of glory in this station's spotted history was its role in *Reds*, Warren Beatty's 1981 biopic of radical American journalist John Reed, co-starring Diane

Keaton. In recent times, a shopping centre has been built under the magnificent glass roof, making use of the otherwise redundant space.

All these changes mean that it is difficult to fully appreciate Príncipe Pío as it was when it was Madrid's second most important mainline station. Enough elements associated with railway architecture remain, though, to make it worth looking at. Spectacular in an understated way, the complex includes some decidedly elegant arches on the Paseo de la Florida side, showing the influence of neo-classical ideas on station architecture. Meanwhile, the

façade mixes classical and art-deco elements, and is flanked by two towers, each topped by a cupola.

Other points of interest in the immediate neighbourhood include the Puerta de San Vicente, a replica of the city gate constructed by the illustrious Francesco Sabatini in the 1770s, and the Campo del Moro (the Moor's Field), which is effectively the front garden of the Palacio Real, a wonderfully quiet, shady park now open to the public and home to many cats.

Below: Colourful trains waiting to depart at Estación de Príncipe Pío

🚩 **17 C4**

✉ **Estación de Príncipe Pío**
Cuesta de San Vicente

☎ 91 758 0040

🌐 www.ccprincipepio.com

🕐 Mon–Thu 10am–1am,
Fri–Sat 10am–2am, Sun
11am–1am

🚇 Príncipe Pío (lines 6, 10
and R)

Jardines de las Vistillas

These tree-filled gardens to the south of the Palacio Real live up to their name (literally "Viewpoint Gardens"), offering splendid views of the Catedral de la Almudena and out across the Casa de Campo and the River Manzanares to the peaks of the Sierra de Guadarrama mountain range.

Occupying shady spots here are small terrace bars, good for an aperitif, a slice of tortilla and a grandstand view of the sunset.

The gardens come into their own during two of the traditional fiesta times, when they are the perfect spot to see Madrileños enjoying themselves as they have for decades. Madrid's patron saint San Isidro celebrates his birthday on 15 May, which also marks the start of the bullfighting season. For a week or so from this date, the gardens are transformed into a bustling late-night party venue with eating, drinking, music and dancing. Families

include the spot on their evening *paseo*, stopping at the many outdoor food stalls to buy piping hot churros or to drink the traditional sangria-like drink, *tinto de verano*. Later on, younger folk flock to the stage set up to dance to the entire range of music contemporary Spain has to offer, from flamenco to rock.

During the months of July and August, las Vistillas is one of many venues across the city to host events for the Veranos de la Villa, the city's summer festival. This festival entails two months of celebrating performances of dances such as tango jazz and flamenco; a form of

Spanish operetta known as *zarzuela*; and the typical Madrileño form of dance music for the popular *chotis*. During these festive times, the gardens are a good place to watch Madrid's *castizos* and *castizas*, the equivalent of London's cockney pearly kings and queens, stepping out in their dapper checked caps, waistcoats and white neckerchiefs. Women may choose a Goya-esque fashion of high hair combs, fringed shawls and full skirts.

When the open-air partying becomes too much, the narrow old medieval streets around the gardens are worth exploring too.

Left: Jardines de las Vistillas

✚ 17 C6

✉ Jardines de las Vistillas
Calle Beatriz Galindo

Ⓜ La Latina

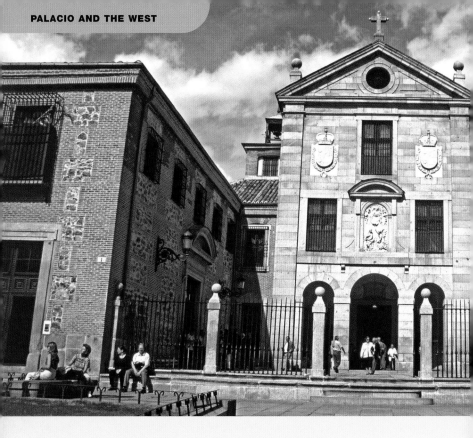

Monasterio de la Encarnación

The Monasterio de la Encarnación, the second of the capital's Hapsburg-endowed monasteries, sits in a quiet square between the Palacio Real and the Plaza de España. It is still home to 20 nuns of the Augustine Recoletos (Augustinian Recollects) order, who stay hidden in their cloisters during visiting hours. It also houses a fascinating reliquary. But is most famous in the city for a yearly phenomenon when crowds line up patiently to see a miracle.

Above left: The grand façade of Monasterio de la Encarnación

On 27 July each year, the solidified blood of Greek martyr San Pantaleón, trapped permanently in a glass orb, liquefies for just one night. Legend has it that the year it doesn't, disaster will ensue.

The blood is part of the extensive reliquary that is the main draw of the convent. Housed in glass cases are around 1,500 artefacts, including slivers of bone and clothing and other belongings of saints and martyrs. Almost of greater interest are the reliquaries that house them – gorgeously jewelled caskets of silver, bronze, gold, marble and fine wood, originating in Germany, Spain and the Netherlands.

The original convent, which was founded in 1611 by Queen Margaret of Austria, wife of Philip III, was built by the architects Juan

Above right: The studded wooden doors set in the walls of the Monasterio de la Encarnación

✚ **17 D4**

✉ **Monasterio de la Encarnación**
Plaza de la Encarnación 1

☎ 91 454 8800

🕐 Tue–Thu and Sat 10:30–12:45, 4–5:45, Fri 10–12:45, Sun 10:30–1:45

✋ Moderate

Ⓜ Ópera or Santo Domingo

Gómez de Mora and Fray Alberto de la Madre de Dios. That building was ravaged by fire in 1734 – all that remains of it is the austere façade. The rest of the monastery was rebuilt by Ventura Rodríguez in a classical baroque style.

The monastery was once a treasury and was connected to the Alcázar (the predecessor of the modern-day royal palace, the Palacio Real – see page 42) by a hidden passageway that royal worshippers used to traverse in order to pass incognito on their way to prayers.

If the monastery itself lacks the atmospheric charm and lavish decoration of its sister, the nearby Monasterio de las Descalzas Reales, it still has a great many things to offer. There is a fine selection of fresco paintings by the González Velásquez brothers and by Francisco Bayeu, a magnificent portrait of John the Baptist by Julepe (José or Jusepe) de Ribera, a valuable collection of 16th- and 17th-century paintings of the Spanish School (regarded as the golden age of Spanish art) and a selection of sculptures.

Also of note are the choir, the cloister, the room of kings and the reliquary chapel, where the blood of San Pantaleón is kept. In front of the building is a statue of the 16th-century poet and playwright Lope de Vega by Mateo Inurria, dating from 1902.

You can only visit here as part of a tour and all tours are conducted solely in Spanish.

Below: A stained glass window depicting Saint Teresa in the Monasterio de la Encarnación, on the northern side of the town of Avila where the saint was born

Muralla Árabe

The Arab armies that occupied much of the southern half of the Iberian peninsula from 711 onwards chose not to move into the hostile and inhospitable lands north of the Sierra de Guadarrama, which is to the north of Madrid. Instead, they fixed a frontier that approximately followed the route of the old Roman road linking Mérida, Toledo and Zaragoza (Saragossa). To defend this frontier from the ever more frequent Christian raids in the 9th century, a series of fortresses was established to the north of this line. Madrid was one of these.

The citadel of Madrid was founded *c*860, during the reign of Mohammed I, the fifth emir of Córdoba. The site for the *qasr*, or fortress, was the hill where the Palacio Real now stands, which afforded good views of the routes heading south from the Guadarrama. The river nearby, now called the Manzanares, and the many springs close to the fort ensured a good supply of water and gave the city its original name, Mayrit, sometimes spelt "Magerit", which in Arabic meant "place of many springs". This later morphed into "Matrit", and from there into "Madrid".

Precious little remains of the Moorish town, which was captured by the Christians in 1086. However, it is clear that it was more than just a fortress, as it had an outer citadel, bounded to the east by the modern-day Calle Factor, and a *medina* (town) delimited by the current Plaza de la Villa and the Calle Segovia. In 1953, excavation uncovered a section of the old flint-stone wall a few yards to the south of the Catedral de la Almudena. The section uncovered is quite small, but is worth visiting as it provides a unique glimpse of a city and a time that has long since been buried and built over.

Above: Muralla Árabe, the archaeological remains of Madrid's Moorish heritage

✚ **17 C5**

✉ **Muralla Árabe**
Cuesta de la Vega s/n

Ⓜ Ópera

Below: An equestrian statue with the tower of the Museo de América rising up in the background

Museo de América

This museum, dedicated to the history, art and culture of the Americas, houses an unbeatable collection of pre-Columbian, Spanish-American and Native American art and artefacts. The collections illustrate the history of America, before and beyond Columbus' discovery of the New World.

Much of the space is given over to the development of the Spanish colonies up to the 19th century, as well as reflections of the history, life and customs of the South and Central American peoples and some pre-Columbian art. While the depth and quality of the pieces is unquestioned, there has been debate over the way they are displayed, using five major themes with classifications such as "Communication" or "The Family", rather than by country or chronology.

That said, there is a wealth of material to enjoy, including the stunning "Treasure of the Quimbayas", a collection of 62 exquisite figures in solid gold presented to Spain by the Columbian government in 1892. Other prestigious acquisitions include textiles and ceremonial garments, including a magnificent feathered cape from Hawaii; Aztec, Mayan and Incan stone sculptures; Peruvian funeral offerings; obsidian masks from Mexico; and finely modelled figurines from the Chibcha culture of Columbia, still as fresh and bursting with life as the day they were made.

One of the museum's most fascinating pieces is the Madrid Codex, thought to date form the 15th century and one of only four illustrated Mayan manuscripts in existence. The Madrid Codex is a single document comprising 56 pages of bark paper, which folds like an accordion and is covered on both sides with Mayan hieroglyphic script and fine illustration. It is thought to originate from the Yucatán Peninsula. It is believed to be the work of eight scribes and to have been sent back to the Spanish royal court by the conquistador Hernán Cortés.

The museum also owns the Tudela Codex, which was produced in the middle of the 16th century, in central Mexico, during the early years of the Spanish conquest. It is interesting not only for its insights into Aztec culture and religion, but for the attached documents – one of which is the "European Written Book", which includes Renaissance-style portraits of indigenous men and women.

The other three are the Dresden, Grolier and Paris codices, named after the cities they came to rest in. The various codices were Mayan almanacs, laying out the ceremonies and rituals of the culture, along with the pantheon of deities, astronomical charts and scenes of everyday life and religious ceremony in pre-Hispanic Mexico – including human sacrifice. These documents were to be found in abundance at the time of the Spanish conquest, but almost all were destroyed by missionaries who feared they were ungodly and who wished to suppress the pagan culture.

✚ **17 C1**

✉ **Museo de América**
Avenida Reyes Católicos 6

☎ 91 549 2641, 91 543 9437

🔳 **http://museodeamerica.mcu.es**

🕐 Tue–Sat 9.30–3, Sun and public hols 10–3

💶 Moderate, free Sun

🚇 Moncloa

Museo Cerralbo

The Museo Cerralbo is the work of love of one fanatical and fastidious collector, Don Enrique de Aguilera y Gamboa, 17th Marqués de Cerralbo (1845–1922). Housed in a sumptuous late 19th-century mansion are more than 50,000 works of art and artefacts, including paintings, sculptures, ceramics, furniture, tapestries, suits of armour and clocks – all the result of a life spent travelling and acquiring.

The marquis was a *diputado* (member of parliament) for the Carlist party by the age of 27. With an aristocratic lineage dating back to the 13th century, any time not spent canvassing he devoted to his other passions, archaeology and collecting. The marquis and his equally enthusiastic collector wife – Doña Manuela Inocencia

Serrano y Cerver – always meant the 25-room mansion to be both house and museum, in the style of grand Italian galleries. To that end, they toured Europe and Asia extensively, scouring auction

Above: The curved façade of the Museo Cerralbo

houses and private collections to amass what was once considered the most exhaustive private collection in the country.

It is a collection of huge breadth and quality, the highlights of which include paintings by Titian, Tintoretto and El Greco, including his classic *Ecstasy of St Francis of Assisi*. Other important Spanish works, dating from the 17th century, include prominent pieces such as Zurbarán's *Immaculate Conception*, the *Pietà* by Alonso Cano and *Saint Dominic in Soriano* by Antonio de Pereda. The collection also includes significant still-life paintings by El Labrador, Gabriel de la Corte and Arellano,

among others. Further delights include 18th-century English watches, Venetian lamps, Saxon porcelain as well as Sèvres,

✚ **17 D4**

✉ **Museo Cerralbo**
Calle Ventura Rodríguez 17

☎ 91 547 3646

🌐 **http://museocerralbo.mcu.es**

🕐 Tue–Sat 9:30–3pm, Sun and public hols 10–3

✋ Moderate

Ⓜ Plaza de España or Ventura Rodríguez

Above left: The library is rich in wood panelling and marble; **above right:** the Salón Imperio

Above left: The lush garden with its many statues; **left:** The ornate carved staircase is by Soriano Fort

Wedgwood and Meissen, and also European and 18th-century Japanese battle armour. The English-style landscape garden features sculptures of mythological figures and busts of Roman emperors.

The marquis, who gave up his political career with the loss of Spain's colonies for a life of horse breeding and farming, died at the mansion in 1922. He bequeathed his entire collection to the state; 40 years later, it was declared a national monument. Part of the museum's charm derives from the fact that in his will, the marquis left strict instructions that the collection "always remain together and be used for study by those devoted to science and art", which means that the layout remains unchanged with dense displays of paintings three deep on the walls.

Apart from its displays, the house itself – with its everyday objects still arrayed as the marquis and his family left them – is a perfect example of a baroque–classical townhouse of the period, laid out in the style of the day, with the private rooms on the mezzanine floor while the reception halls and entertainment rooms are on the main floor. It offers a fascinating glimpse into the life of a 19th-century Spanish aristocrat – strolling through the formal dining room, lavish ballroom, reception rooms, kitchens and coach houses, it is easy to conjure up a life of literary gatherings and balls.

The museum is currently closed for renovation work and it is scheduled to reopen in 2009.

Above centre: A display of swords on the third floor; **above right:** Museo Cerralbo's Salita Rosa; **right:** Comedor de Gala, the grand dining room

Museo del Traje

One of Madrid's newest museums, the Museo del Traje (Museum of Clothing) was inaugurated in 2004, though the collections held there had existed under various names and been exhibited in different venues since the mid-1920s.

It is situated in an early-1970s building that formerly housed the Spanish Museum of Contemporary Art, whose collections were absorbed by the Museo Nacional Centro de Arte Reina Sofía in 1990. Its future at the present site is in doubt, however, as the lease on the land on which the museum stands comes up for review in 2013 and the proprietor, the Universidad Complutense de Madrid (UCM), may want to use it for its own projects.

For the time being, however, anyone interested in the history of fashion will not be disappointed by the Museo del Traje. On show is a permanent exhibition covering six centuries of Spanish apparel; plus many older items, including fragments of Coptic cloth and pieces from the Hispanic-Muslim period. There are frequent temporary shows as well, and a showcase called "Treasures of the Past", in which ancient pieces on loan from other institutions are exhibited for six months at a time. In terms of the permanent exhibits, there is no guarantee as to exactly what visitors will actually see at any given time, as many items in the 160,000-piece collection are extremely fragile and are thus rotated for their protection. This does mean that returning visitors may see other items, and therefore appreciate the collection's range and diversity all the more.

The museum comprises 14 chronological and monographic sections. Outstanding among them are the room with regional costumes and that dedicated to the creations of Mariano Fortuny y Madrazo, whose clothes were worn by, among others, Isadora Duncan. There are also the rooms covering clothing from the times of the Enlightenment, *castizo* clothes as worn by Madrid's traditional working class, garments of the Romantic period and the *belle époque*, fashion from the post-Civil War period and the modern era. Another room shows pieces by the great Spanish designer Balenciaga, while there is also one that looks at haute couture.

In a "didactic area", visitors can learn about the processes by which clothes are made. There is also a bookshop, a café-style restaurant and an internet/reading room.

Left: Costumes worn at Spanish festivals are brightly coloured and beautifully detailed, such as this one worn at the Fiesta de San Mateo

---

✠ **17 B1**

✉ **Museo del Traje**
Avenida Juan de Herrera 2

☎ 91 550 4700

🕐 Tue–Sat 9.30–7, Sun 10–3

✋ Inexpensive, free Sat afternoon and Sun

Ⓜ Moncloa

Palacio Real

A magnificent baroque pile of granite and white Colmenar stone, the Palacio Real is the official residence of King Juan Carlos and the Spanish royal family. However, the palace is now used by them only for public functions, such as the 2004 wedding banquet of Prince Felipe. It was last lived in as a royal residence in 1931, before King Alfonso XIII and his wife Victoria Eugenia fled Spain.

Reflecting the former glory of the House of Bourbon, the Palacio Real sits with its east façade dominating the Plaza de Oriente (see page 52) and the west looking out over the Campo del Moro (see page 28). Owned now by the Spanish state, the palace is the largest in Western Europe. (Juan Carlos and his family live comparatively modestly in

Above left: The splendid interior of Palacio Real; **above right:** Changing of the Guard

✚ **17 D5**

✉ **Palacio Real**
Calle de Bailén

☎ 91 454 8800

🕐 Apr–Sep Mon–Sat 9:30–6; Oct–Mar Mon–Sat 9:30–5, Sun and public holidays 9–2

✋ Expensive

🎭 Ópera

the Palacio de la Zarzuela on the outskirts of Madrid.)

The Palacio Real occupies an area of 135,000sq m (0.05sq miles) and has almost 3,000 rooms (50 of which are open to the public), 870 windows, 240 balconies, 44 sets of stairs and 110 doors.

The origins of the site date back to the 9th century, when a fortress was built during the Islamic kingdom and later appropriated by the kings of Castile. A new palace was commissioned by Philip V to replace the Alcázar fortress after it was destroyed by fire in 1734. Italian architects Francesco Sabatini and Giambattista Sacchetti came up with the final design for a building which was to be made entirely of stone and brick, and thus safe from fire. Construction lasted from

1738 to 1755, with the finished structure facing onto the Plaza de Armas and later towards the Catedral de la Almudena. King Charles III took up residence in 1764.

The interior can be viewed on a fixed-itinerary tour and boasts a series of spectacular rooms packed with art treasures and antiques, including priceless collections of porcelain, tapestries, rock-crystal chandeliers, gilt and bronze mirrors and

Left: Guards standing to attention outside Palacio Real; **above:** Many magnificent statues line the path leading to the palace

Above: The Palacio Real seen in all its splendour from the Campo del Moro

clocks as well as the world's only complete Stradivarius quartet.

The tour begins at the jaw-droppingly grand main staircase leading up to the main state rooms. Unmissable among these is the Throne Room, preserved intact from the reign of King Charles III, with a ceiling fresco depicting the Spanish monarchy painted by Giovanni Battista (Giambattista) Tiepolo. It is furnished with carved gilt furniture and velvet wall hangings featuring embroidery from Naples. The enormous mirrors were manufactured in the royal glass factory of La Granja and the rock-crystal chandeliers come from Venice. The bronze lions flanking the dais were brought from Rome by Velázquez, who also commissioned the 17th-century sculptures that were saved from the ruined Alcázar.

The private chambers are just as gorgeously decked out. Best among them are the King's Chamber (or Gasparini Room) and the Porcelain Room, a masterly use of the medium as wall relief, produced by the royal factory at Buen Retiro.

The state dining room, a later addition, is still used for official functions. Of special note are the Royal Pharmacy and the Royal Armoury. The Pharmacy, accessed through separate entrances, has its walls lined with blue-and-white potion jars and paintings of the men entrusted with the royal family's health. The Armoury is said to hold one of the most important collections of weapons in the world, with royal suits of armour

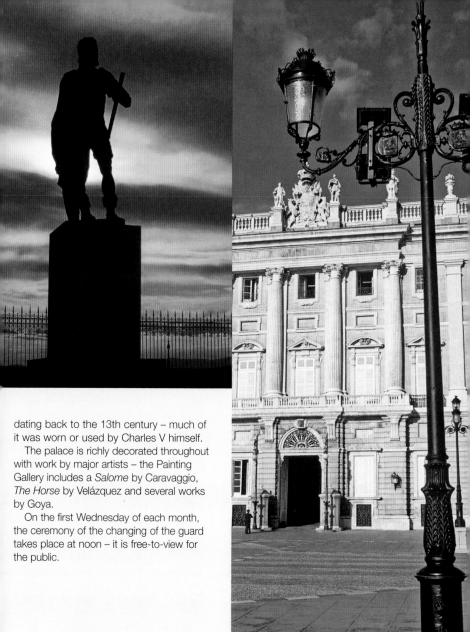

dating back to the 13th century – much of it was worn or used by Charles V himself.

The palace is richly decorated throughout with work by major artists – the Painting Gallery includes a *Salome* by Caravaggio, *The Horse* by Velázquez and several works by Goya.

On the first Wednesday of each month, the ceremony of the changing of the guard takes place at noon – it is free-to-view for the public.

Above: The statue of Alfonso II, silhouetted against an orange sky as the sun sets beyond and between merlons on Palacio Real; **right:** The façade of Palacio Real on Plaza de Oriente

Parque del Oeste

The gorgeous Parque del Oeste (West Park) was commissioned in 1906 by then-mayor Alberto Aguilera, and was designed and laid out by the master gardener Cecilio Rodríguez. When Madrid was besieged by Franco's nationalist forces during the Spanish Civil War, the park was part of the front line and as a result was laid waste. Since then it has been completely relaid and is now a beautifully landscaped haven of shade and tranquillity only minutes from the hustle and bustle of central Madrid.

The park can be accessed from many points, one of which is the Plaza de España. Stretching northwest from the Plaza de España, it is bounded to the west by a railway line from and to the east by the Calle de Ferraz and its continuation, the Paseo del Pintor Rosales.

On crossing the Calle de Ferraz, you cannot fail to see a stone structure that seems, at first, a little incongruous. It is an Egyptian temple, the Templo de Debod. This temple dates from the early 2nd century BC and was initially built as a small chapel dedicated to the gods Amon and

Isis. It was later enlarged by various kings of the Ptolemaic dynasty and then by the Roman emperors Augustus, Tiberius and, possibly, Hadrian. The Egyptian government donated the temple to Spain in 1968 in return for the Spanish government's cooperation in the saving of many monuments that would otherwise have been engulfed by the rising waters after the construction of the Aswan Dam.

Another way to the park is via Calle Marqués de Urquijo, from Argüelles. This brings you out opposite the Teleférico station. The Teleférico is a cable car that leaves from here and takes you on an 11-minute ride deep into the Casa de Campo.

Along the wide pavement of the Paseo del Pintor Rosales are several outdoor cafés where you can take refreshment before or after visiting the park. The Parque del Oeste spreads over a hillside – venture down to the bottom where there is another feature that is worth visiting: the Rosaleda, a magnificent rose garden laid out in 1958.

Above left: The reconstructed remains of the Egyptian Templo de Debod, in the Parque del Oeste; **above right:** The Rosaleda rose garden

✚ **17 B2**

✉ **Parque del Oeste**
   Paseo del Pintor Rosales

🚇 Argüelles or Plaza de España

Plaza de España

Encircled by towering office blocks and snarling traffic at the western end of central Madrid's main artery (the Gran Vía), the Plaza de España offers a much-needed opportunity for workers and tourists alike to rest tired feet. Designed by Teodoro Anasagasti and Mateo Inurria, this large, pleasant green with pool and fountain was established on the site of a former barracks.

It became a popular public square in the 1950s with the building of its two landmark skyscrapers – the Edificio España and the Torre de Madrid – by the brothers Julián and José María Otamendi.

There is another draw for tourists: the plaza is a popular photo spot thanks to the monument to Spain's most famous author and his even more famous creations, which stands at its centre. A stone statue of novelist, poet and playwright Miguel de Cervantes Saavedra looks down benignly on that most engagingly odd couple – Don Quixote and Sancho Panza, rendered in bronze.

Nearby are two stone sculptures of two others of Cervantes' characters, the peasant woman Aldonza Lorenzo and the beautiful figment of the thin knight's imagination, Dulcinea del Toboso.

The monument was designed by architects Pedro Muguruza and Rafael Martínez Zapatero, executed by sculptor Lorenzo Coullaut Valera. Much of the work was carried out between 1925 and 1930, with the son of the sculptor, Federico Coullaut-Valera Mendigutía, finishing the job in 1957.

The two skyscrapers, which were once the highest buildings in the city, have long since slipped down the ratings and are now positively dwarfed by the Cuatro Torres Business Area (CTBA) to the north of Plaza Castilla. The Edificio España, one of Madrid's most emblematic buildings, has fallen on even harder times. Constructed by the Otamendis between 1948 and 1953, the neo-baroque building with its distinctive 117m (384-foot), 28-storey tower flanked by two stepped terraces was once home to the Crowne Plaza Hotel, restaurants, shops swimming pool and 500 office workers; but it is now empty. Bought by a part of the Santander banking group in 2005, it languishes without purpose now – but it is still held in great affection by Madrileños, who wouldn't recognise their city without it.

Far left: The monument to Cervantes and the statues of Don Quixote at Plaza de España; **below:** A classic Spanish shop window display

✚ **17 D4**

✉ **Plaza de España**
End of Gran Vía

✋ Free

🚇 Plaza de España

PLAZA DE ORIENTE

Plaza de Oriente

Translating as "East Square", Madrid's most elegant square often has map readers wondering why it is called that despite being in the west of the city. Actually, the Plaza de Oriente takes its name from the fact it is positioned to the east of the Palacio Real. Given the harmony of the royal palace, the neat gardens bracketed by crescents of apartments, it is hard to believe that this square was not one big Bourbon project.

However, it was in fact Joseph Bonaparte, brother of Napoleon, who – during his brief reign from 1808 to 1813 – initiated work on the square, knocking down dwellings and convents to clear the space. The work was never completed on quite the scale he had imagined, but city dwellers were given a cool, elegant space in which to promenade. Today it is the spot for elegant matrons to enjoy an aperitif, and

D. SANCHA
REINA DE LEON
Mª Aª DE 1000

its benches and gardens are filled with tourists and courting couples alike.

The walkways through the gardens are lined with statues of the country's kings and queens through the ages, but look carefully and many appear crude or unfinished. This is because they were originally designed to be mounted on the palace and viewed from afar, but proved dangerously heavy and so were left in the square.

In the centre of the plaza is a fine bronze statue of King Philip IV mounted on a rearing horse. The statue, created by Italian sculptor Pietro Tacca and originally placed in the Palacio del Buen Retiro, is unusual in that the animal is supported on its rear legs.

Above left: Ornate façade, Plaza de Oriente; **above right:** The square is lined with statues of Spanish rulers

✚ **17 D5**

✉ **Plaza de Oriente**
Plaza de Oriente

✋ Free

🚇 Ópera

Galileo Galilei, no less, was brought in to tackle the problem of physics that balances it in so odd a position – he solved it by making the front of the horse hollow and the hindquarters solid.

Sitting massively between the two crescents of housing opposite the Royal Palace is the royal opera house, the Teatro Real. Since its opening in 1850, the opera house has been bugged by lack of funds, fire and even a gunpowder explosion – it closed its doors altogether in the 1980s for extensive refurbishment. It is now one of the most technologically sophisticated opera houses in Europe.

On either side of the opera building are two highly popular establishments – the Café de Oriente and the Taberna del Alabardero are thronged by patrons eager to soak up the atmosphere on fine days, and try the seriously good Spanish food on offer. The café and restaurant are both part of the hugely successful Lezama group, owned by a Jesuit padre – his chain of restaurants extends to America and the profits are ploughed into charitable enterprises.

The square has its dark side too – for older Madrileños, it is inextricably linked to Franco, who held all his biggest rallies here. Even now, on 20 November, the

anniversary of his death, an ever-dwindling group of fur-coated grande dames and their husbands gather to raise their arms in the Fascist salute.

To fully experience the plaza, a stroll at night – when the lamps are lit and youngsters gather under the statue of Philip IV to chat and sing – is well worth it.

Above: Café de Oriente in Plaza de Oriente; **right:** An equestrian statue of Philip IV in Plaza de Oriente

San Nicolás de los Servitas

A short walk from the Plaza de Oriente, the Iglesia de San Nicolás de los Servitas is Madrid's oldest church. The bell tower is thought to date back to the 12th century, and is certainly one of only two surviving Mudéjar-style towers surviving in Madrid. The other is to be found at San Pedro el Viejo (see page 98).

There is some debate as to whether the tower was actually built during Muslim rule, therefore forming part of a mosque, or whether it was in fact constructed later by Muslim craftsmen under Christian rule, or even by Spanish workers who had learned to build in that style. Whatever the truth is, it most certainly resembles a minaret, complete with horseshoe and lobe arches – well worth taking a look at.

The rest of the church is more recent, having been constructed in the 15th century, with a fine central apse built in the Gothic style. Indeed, there have been several later additions over the centuries.

The church survived a bombing during the Civil War, though it was restored shortly afterwards, a project which brought to light various decorative elements that had long been covered up in the presbytery. The chapels inside the church contain an interesting collection of paintings and sculptures by Catholic missionary Juan María Salvatierra, Pedro de Mena and Nicolás Busi, as well as some of the most impressive coffered ceilings in Madrid.

The opening times given here are approximate guidelines. To visit the church outside those times, visitors can go to the priory on the Travesía del Biombo, the little street behind the church, and request the monks to open it (they are generally quite amenable).

Right: The bell tower of San Nicolás de los Servitas

 17 D5

✉ **San Nicolás de los Servitas**
Plaza San Nicolás

☎ 91 559 4064

🕐 Tue–Sat 9–9:30am, 6:30–8:30pm, Sun 10–2, 6:30–8:30, Mon 8:30am–1pm

✋ Free

Ⓜ Ópera

Viaducto

The Calle de Segovia runs down an ancient watercourse between two hills. On one of them stand the Palacio Real and the Catedral de la Almudena; across, on the other side, is the Jardines de las Vistillas and nearby the Austrias neighbourhood. Linking these two areas was long an obsession of Madrid's architects and mayors. This viaduct was eventually built in 1872, based on a project by Enrique Barron.

It was a metal structure that was in need of replacing by the late 1920s. The replacement – the work of a team of architects – was initiated in 1932. The result is the magnificent rationalist, reinforced-concrete structure that still stands today, comprising three arches, each with a span of 35m (115 feet) and a rise of 17.5m (about 58 feet).

Though it was closed to traffic in 1975 and indeed was on the point of being demolished, the viaduct was saved and restored between 1975 and 1978. Today the viaduct is one of Madrid's most recognisable landmarks. It is worth taking your time crossing it to appreciate the fabulous views over the Casa de Campo and the Guadarrama Mountains in the distance.

It is also famous amongst Madrileños as being a popular suicide spot, success being more or less assured when jumping from such a height. This explains the installation of perspex screens in the early 1990s that, while not enhancing the views, do act as a deterrent to those wishing to end it all in this way. Legend has it that a young woman threw herself off the original viaduct in the late 19th century because her family would not allow her to marry the young man of her choice. While plunging to a certain death, the young lady's skirt got entangled in the structure, breaking her fall and saving her life. She eventually died many years later, after having 14 children, though it is not known whether the father was her chosen beau.

Left: Madrid's tree-lined Calle de Segovia, with the vast arched Viaducto above

✚ **17 D5**

✉ **Viaducto**
Calle de Bailén

🚇 Ópera

Centro

Madrid is one of the most compelling cities in Europe and a lot of the fascination lies within the confines of its vibrant city centre. El Centro contains areas of great historical interest such as the 16th-century Plaza Mayor and old Madrid (Madrid de los Austrias), and these very sites feature many of the bars and restaurants that contribute to Madrid having arguably some of the best nightlife in Europe. So why not start your tour of the Centro over a glass of wine and a *tapa* in the Plaza Mayor and contemplate the spectacular architecture?

CENTRO WALK

1. Real Academia de Bellas Artes de San Fernando
See page 94

Take the southern exit from the Banco de España metro station and walk up Calle de Alcalá. You will pass the spectacular Círculo de Bellas Artes arts centre on your left, with its stylish café. Cross the road and continue along Calle de Alcalá for approximately 230m (250 yards) until you reach the Real Academia de Bellas Artes, which houses one of the most important art collections in the country, including 13 works by Goya.

2. Puerta del Sol
See page 88

Turn right out of the Real Academia and you will find bustling Sol, the heart of Madrid. Continue westwards and you will pass a monument featuring the emblems of Madrid – a bear under a *madroño* tree. Directly opposite is Casa de Correos and the Kilómetro Cero. Head west on Calle Mayor.

3. Plaza Mayor
See page 82

Take a left turn along the bustling Calle de Postas and enter the magnificent 17th-century Plaza Mayor with its grey slate roofs, pinnacles and statue of Philip III. Once the scene of executions and bullfights, it now contains a thriving Sunday stamp and coin market, and is a popular outdoor concert venue.

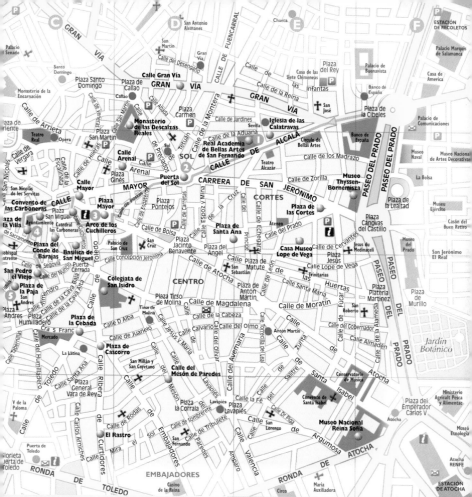

4. Plaza de la Villa
See page 87

Take the southwest exit from the Plaza Mayor and walk down the steps under the Arco de Cuchilleros. Turn right up Cava de San Miguel and continue westwards along Calle Mayor until you reach Madrid's oldest square – Plaza de la Villa, which boasts three differing architectural styles and contains the Casa de la Villa.

5. Plaza de la Paja
See page 85

Exit Plaza de la Villa from the 16th-century Casa de Cisneros and walk along Calle del Cordón until you reach Calle de Segovia. Walk up the steps and turn right along Calle del Nuncio, passing Iglesia de San Pedro el Viejo. Turn along Calle Príncipe Anglona to reach the pretty Plaza de la Paja, formerly a medieval corn market.

Arco de Cuchilleros

The southwest corner of the Plaza Mayor is known as the Arco de Cuchilleros. It is so called because the archway leads down a flight of steps to the Calle de Cuchilleros, or 'knife-grinders' street', where knife and sword makers were based. These days, bustling Cuchilleros is a favourite with tavern hoppers and tourists.

Formerly known as the Calle de la Escalerilla de Piedra or 'street of the stone steps', the Arco de Cuchilleros was a key setting in Pérez Galdós's celebrated 19th-century novel *Fortunata y Jacinta*. It is also the site of a fire which devastated half of the Plaza Mayor in 1790.

If you walk down the stone steps, you will encounter a gentleman in early-19th-century costume brandishing a blunderbuss. He is the doorman for Las Cuevas de Luis Candelas, which is one of Madrid's oldest taverns and is named after the city's notorious 19th-century bandit Luis Candelas.

Basílica de San Miguel

The imposing Basílica de San Miguel is located in the Calle San Justo on the site of a Romanesque church, which was originally dedicated to two child martyrs, Justo and Pastor. It was built for the youngest son of Philip V – Don Luis de Borbón y Farnesio, who was the Archbishop of Toledo from the age of five.

Designed and constructed between 1739 and 1746 by various architects, including the Italian Giacomo Bonavia, its baroque style marks a sharp contrast with

Above left: Gate of the Plaza Mayor, looking towards Arco de Cuchilleros; **left:** Basílica de San Miguel on Plaza Mayor

the surrounding architecture of old Madrid. The beautiful convex façade boasts four statues representing Faith, Hope, Charity and Strength, and also carvings of Justo and Pastor. The interior of the church, with its single nave, is truly impressive. The decor is mainly 18th century, but a number of the paintings and stained-glass windows are recent.

The Basílica de San Miguel is run by the Opus Dei, and in fact many of its events are held place here. A chapel has been named after the Spanish founder of the organisation, San Escrivá de Balaguer.

Calle Arenal

Arenal (literally "sandy ground") was originally a stream, which became an area of sandy ground during periods of drought. It developed into a busy thoroughfare that linked Sol and the Palacio Real, and acquired a certain prestige following the opening of the Teatro Real in 1850, the year a statue of Isabel II was placed on the east side of the theatre.

The Teatro Real has been renovated on several occasions, most recently in 1991–7. It has an imposing, austere façade that belies its richly decorated interior, and is one of the most technologically advanced opera houses in Europe.

Walk east along Arenal and you'll pass the Iglesia de San Ginés, whose origins date back to the 12th century. In the adjoining alley, you will discover the Chocolatería San Ginés, which serves chocolate and *churros*, and is a favourite with night owls looking for a sugar and caffeine hit after a hard night's clubbing.

At Arenal 9 is the splendid Palacio Gaviria, concealed behind a modern façade. Built by the Marqués de Gaviria in 1851 to receive Isabel II, it is now a club and a popular venue for parties and receptions.

Right: Shoppers milling around the stores on Calle Arenal

Arco de Cuchilleros

✚ **61 C2**

✉ **Arco de Cuchilleros**
Plaza Mayor

🚇 Sol

Basílica de San Miguel

✚ **61 C2**

✉ **Basílica de San Miguel**
Calle San Justo 4

☎ 91 548 4011

🕐 18 Sep–30 Jun daily 9:45–2, 5:30–9; 1 Jul– 17 Sep daly 10:15–1, 6–9

🚇 Sol

Calle Arenal

✚ **61 D2**

✉ **Calle del Arenal**
Calle Arenal

🚇 Sol and Ópera

Calle Mayor

This road connects two gates in the medieval city wall, the Puerta de la Vega (near Cuesta de la Vega) and Puerta de Guadalajara, located near Plaza del Comandante Las Morenas. Calle Mayor has thus long been the preferred route for religious processions and festive parades.

Calle Mayor borders two of Madrid's most emblematic squares – Plaza Mayor, near the bustling Puerta del Sol, and Plaza de la Villa, near the Palacio Real in the west. Plaza de la Villa is Madrid's oldest square – dating from early Muslim times. Originally a market square, it became an exclusive residential area during the pre-Habsburg period. The oldest building in the square is the 15th-century Torre de los Lujanes, which stands opposite the 17th-century Casa de la Villa, which until recently was the Madrid City Hall.

If you walk in an easterly direction towards Sol, you will pass the only surviving wrought-iron market building in the metropolis – the Mercado de San Miguel, which was built between 1913 and 1916. Before entering the Plaza Mayor, take a look at the sloping outside walls of the square on your right, which house several warren-like *mesónes* or taverns.

Enter the 17th-century Plaza Mayor by the northeast entrance. On your left is the Casa de la Panadería (the bakers' guild), which is the oldest and most ornate section of the Plaza Mayor. Formerly the scene of executions and bullfights, the square is still an occasional outdoor concert venue. Contemplate the grey slate roofs and pinnacles designed by Juan Gómez de Mora from one of the numerous café terraces that line the square.

Calle del Mesón de Paredes

Formerly known as Calle Mesón, few streets conjure up such potent images of *castizo* Madrid as this narrow, one-way thoroughfare that rolls downhill from Plaza de Tirso de Molina.

Its present name, since 1835, honours Simón Miguel Paredes, the owner of a huge tavern located at the top of the street.

The street has undergone a drastic transformation during the past decade and has lost most of its old bars and restaurants. Recent Chinese, Moroccan and West African immigrants now give the area a multicultural feel and the street is lined with wholesale clothes shops, kebab joints, halal butchers and Arab tea shops.

But some of the old feel remains. At the top end of the street is one bar that has remained largely unchanged – Casa Mariano. Mariano Herrero, the bar's original owner, founded Real Madrid's first ever supporters' club here in 1920. The bar is still festooned with club memorabilia and players' photographs.

Calle Mayor

✚ **61 C2**

✉ **Calle Mayor**
Calle Mayor

🚇 Sol and Ópera

Calle del Mesón de Paredes

✚ **61 D4**

✉ **Calle del Mesón de Paredes**
Calle del Mesón de Paredes

🚇 Tirso de Molina

Left: A set of painted tiles depicting a rural scene on the frontage of a shop on Calle Mayor

Casa Museo de Lope de Vega

In Calle Cervantes, a quiet street in Madrid's Letras (literary) neighbourhood, you will find the simple house where Félix Lope de Vega Carpio lived. Lope de Vega was Spain's most prolific Golden-Age writer – he is believed to have written somewhere in the region of 2,000 plays. He moved here in 1610 and stayed until his death in 1635, when the city was thrown into great mourning.

It was during this period that he wrote over two thirds of his work, including some of his most famous plays – such as *Peribáñez, Fuente Ovejuna* and *El Caballero de Olmedo*.

The brick-fronted, three-storey house was restored in 1935 and converted into a museum. The aim of the museum was to maintain the original austere decoration of the period, using 17th-century furniture and ornaments, some of which belonged to Lope de Vega himself. The house is built around a small garden containing fruit trees and plants that Lope de Vega frequently referred to in his works.

Colegiata de San Isidro

This huge church with its baroque twin towers is one of the most striking features of Calle Toledo. It was built in 1622 by Pedro Sánchez, on the lines of the Chiesa del Sacro Nome di Gesù in Rome (the mother church of the Society of Jesus or Jesuits).

Above: A portrait of Lope de Vega on the walls of his former home, now open as a museum; **right:** Colegiata de San Isidro seen from Plaza Mayor

The Colegiata originally comprised a Jesuit church and school, which was attended by many of the Golden Age playwrights, including Lope de Vega and Calderón de la Barca. After Sánchez died, Francisco Bautista constructed the large slate dome and completed the façade.

Following the expulsion of the Jesuits from Spain in 1768 by Charles III, the church and college became two separate entities. The church was bestowed with the name 'San Isidro' and restored by Ventura Rodríguez to house the remains of the saint and his wife, which were previously in the Capilla de San Isidro. The church was then returned to the Jesuits under Fernando VII.

It became Madrid's 'temporary' cathedral between 1885 and 1993, at which point the Catedral de la Almudena was completed and took over the honour.

Convento de las Carboneras

The Convento del Corpus Christi (convent of the nuns of Corpus Christi) of Madrid is popularly known as the Convento de las Carboneras, or Convent of the Charcoal Makers. Legend has it that in the late 17th century, some children found a painting in a coal heap and dragged it along the street towards the present-day Plaza del Conde de Miranda. A passing monk realised it was a painting of the Virgin and ensured it was donated to the convent.

If you walk along Calle Codo (literally 'Elbow Street', as it has a sharp bend) from Plaza de la Villa, you reach the Plaza del Conde de Miranda. On the right lies the convent. Founded in 1607 by Beatriz Ramírez de Mendoza, the convent belongs to the Hieronymite order. The painting from the charcoal pile now hangs opposite the main entrance.

The convent is closed to the public. Until recently, it was possible to gain partial access to the convent by means of a revolving window, called a *torno*, to buy cakes and biscuits baked by the nuns. This practice seems to have been discontinued, regrettably.

Casa Museo de Lope de Vega

✚ **61 E2**

✉ **Casa Museo de Lope de Vega**
Calle Cervantes 11

☎ 91 429 9216

🕓 Tue–Sat 9:30–1:30 (but check renovation schedule)

✋ Inexpensive

🚇 Antón Martín

Colegiata de San Isidro

✚ **61 C3**

✉ **Colegiata de San Isidro**
Calle Toledo 37

☎ 91 369 2037

🕓 Sep–Jul daily 7:45–12:30, 6–8:30; Aug Mon–Sat 7:30–8:30, Sun 8:30–1:30, 7:15–8:30

✋ Free

🚇 La Latina

Convento de las Carboneras

✚ **61 C2**

✉ **Convento de las Carboneras**
Plaza del Conde de Miranda

🚇 Sol

Gran Vía

In the late 19th century, as Madrid's middle class grew rapidly, the need for a modern main street that would connect the Plaza de Cibeles and Calle Princesa was felt. Some 14 streets were demolished to carve out this "great way", which was eventually inaugurated by King Alfonso XIII in 1906.

Construction continued over a number of years, in three phases. The aim was to make the Calle Gran Vía as ostentatious as possible after neutral Madrid became prosperous during World War I, when it was the clearing house for foreign capital.

Perhaps the most elegant section was the first to be built, which runs from Calle de Alcalá to the Red de San Luis. Buildings of note here include the Edificio Metrópolis and the Edificio Grassy, both of which have circular towers.

The French-style Edificio Metrópolis, on the corner of Gran Vía and Alcalá, is one of Madrid's most emblematic buildings, with its dark grey slate dome and gilt decor topped with a statue to Winged Victory. It was built by the designers Jules and Raymond Février for the Union and Fenix Español insurance company.

Another Madrid landmark not to be missed in this section is the Museo Chicote – an art deco cocktail bar that was a favourite haunt of celebrities such as Ernest Hemingway, Ava Gardner and Frank Sinatra.

About 100m (110 yards) to the west stands the 1920s Manhattan-style Telefónica building, which was the brainchild of the American architect Louis S Weeks. Boasting an 81metre (266-feet) high tower, it was Madrid's highest building and provided the ideal vantage point for the besieged Republicans to survey the Nationalists during the Spanish Civil War.

By contrast, only yards away, the Plaza de Callao features a number of art-deco edifices that were originally built as cinemas.

Construction of the last section of the Gran Vía, which goes as far as Plaza de España, was completed between 1922 and 1925.

Below: Junction of Gran Vía and Calle de Alcalá – on the left is the Edificio Metrópolis, and tucked in just behind it, with the cupola like a wedding cake on top, is the Edificio Grassy

✚ **61 D1**

✉ **Gran Vía**
Calle Gran Vía

Ⓜ Gran Vía, Santo Domingo and Plaza de España

Iglesia de las Calatravas

Formerly known as the Monasterio Real de la Concepción, the origins of this church date back to 1623, when the nuns of the military order of Calatrava moved to Madrid from Almonacid de Zorita in Guadalajara. They took up residence in a convent in Calle Santa Isabel and lived for a period of time at the end of Calle Atocha. They moved to this convent church at the end of the 17th century.

The church of the Calatravas is located on Alcalá, on the corner of Calle Sevilla and Virgen de los Peligros. It is just one of a number of grandiose buildings that lines Alcalá between Plaza de Cibeles and Sol.

The original convent was given an order for demolition during the 1868 revolution, when Isabel II was ousted from the throne. However, it was saved following some fierce campaigning by the lawyer and politician Manuel Silvela, although legend has it that it was saved due to the intervention of General Prim's wife.

The building was constructed between 1670 and 1678, according to plans drawn up by the Augustinian monk Lorenzo de San Nicolás. It was later completed by Isidro Martínez and Gregorio Garrote. The church, which is essentially baroque in style, boasts a spectacular slate dome set on an octagonal tambour that features four open windows and four bricked-in windows. It also boasts a rose window with the cross of Calatrava.

The original façade was renovated in the mid-19th century by Juan de Madrazo, who was inspired by Milanese architecture. Renovation included applying terracotta to the façade and incorporating neo-Renaissance decor. One of the most striking features is the elaborate altarpiece by José Benito de Churriguera, which was created between 1720 and 1724, with polychrome figures by Pablo González Velásquez.

Above: The interior of the Iglesia de las Calatravas

✠ **61 E1**

✉ **Iglesia de las Calatravas**
Calle de Alcalá 25

☎ 91 521 8035

🕐 Daily 8–1 and 6–8

🚶 Free

Ⓜ Sevilla

Monasterio de las Descalzas Reales

Head down Postigo de San Martín from the bustling Plaza de Callao and you will soon discover an old brick building on your left. This is the Monasterio de las Descalzas Reales, one of the few remaining examples of 16th-century architecture in the capital. This convent has seen and survived numerous wars, uprisings and fires.

Formerly a medieval palace, the building was converted into a convent by Antonio Sillero and Juan Bautista de Toledo around 1560, when Philip II's sister, Juana de Austria, was widowed and decided to take the vows. The Descalzas Reales then became the chosen convent for other female members of the aristocracy who wished do the same. Over the years, the convent frequently received visits from eminent royal visitors, and until the 18th

century, the bodies of departed kings and princes were brought here to receive their last rites.

The convent still accommodates a number of Franciscan nuns who are not allowed to communicate with the outside world. However, despite this being a cloistered order, a section of the building has been converted into a museum that exhibits a veritable wealth of treasures – paintings, sculptures and tapestries –

that were generously donated by the families of the novices.

The interior is decorated in the baroque style, with a magnificent painted staircase that has survived from the original palace. There are 17th-century ceiling frescoes by José Ximénez Donoso and Claudio Coello, and a fresco of Philip IV and family by Antonio de Pereda. The staircase leads to an upper cloister, which is surrounded by chapels that contain objets d'art donated by former nuns on entering the order. Originally a dormitory, the Gran Sala de Tapices (the tapestry room) displays a number of tapestries that were donated to the convent by the Infanta Isabel Clara Eugenia.

The art collection features works by Italian painters such as Titian, Bernardino Luini and Angelo Nardi as well as Flemish painters such as Breughel (*The Adoration of the Magi*) and Rubens. Examples of Spanish baroque religious art, including paintings by Zurbarán, Claudio Coello and Goya are also on show.

✚ **61 D1**

✉ **Monasterio de las Descalzas Reales**
Plaza de las Descalzas 3

☎ 91 454 8800

🔳 **www.patrimonionacional.es/en/descreal/descreal.htm**

🕐 Tue–Thu, Sat 10:30–12:30, 4–5:45, Fri 10:30–12:45, Sun and public hols 11–1:45

💶 Inexpensive

Ⓜ Callao

Above left: The monastery's unassuming brick front; **above right:** A fresco depicting the life of St Francis in the chapter house of the monastery

Museo Nacional Reina Sofía

The Museo Nacional Reina Sofía is housed in the 18th-century Hospital General de San Carlos, the building of which was initiated by Hermosilla under Fernando VI and continued by Sabatini during Charles III's reign.

The hospital was shut down in 1965 and there were actually plans to demolish the building. Luckily, it was declared to be of historic and cultural interest in 1977. In 1980 Antonio Fernández Alba began restoring the interior.

The museum finally opened in 1986, initially with temporary exhibitions on the ground and first floors. The final touches were added in 1988 by José Luis Iñiguez de Onzoño and Antonio Vázquez de Castro, including the impressive glass-and-steel lift shafts on the outside of the building that were a collaborative project with British architect Ian Richie. Since 2005, the rear of the building has featured an equally

impressive extension by French architect Jean Nouvel in the shape of three glass-and-steel edifices topped by a triangular zinc-and-aluminium roof.

The main attraction at the Reina Sofía has to be Picasso's *Guernica*. Picasso was commissioned to produce a mural for the Spanish pavilion at the Paris Exhibition of 1937. He was originally unsure what to paint, but the destruction of the Basque town Guernica by Nazi bombers who supported Franco provided him with the ideal subject matter. Picasso would not allow *Guernica* to be shown in Spain until the restoration of democracy. Franco died in 1975; in 1981, the painting was shipped to Spain from the New York Museum of Art to the Casón del Buen Retiro, which was

Above left: Visitors at the Museo Nacional Reina Sofía admire Picasso's *Guernica*, painted in protest after the bombing of Guernica during the Spanish Civil War; **above right:** The museum's courtyard seen from its glass lift

✠ **61 F4**

✉ **Museo Nacional Reina Sofía**
Calle Santa Isabel 52

☎ 91 774 1000

ᴡᴡᴡ **www.museoreinasofia.es**

🕑 Mon, Wed–Sat 10–9, Sun 10–2:30, closed Tue

✋ Moderate

🚇 Atocha

then an annex of the Prado Museum and probably the ideal location in Picasso's eyes – he had hoped it would be placed near Velázquez's paintings in the Prado itself. However, *Guernica* was finally transferred in 1992 to what was considered to be a more suitable location, the Reina Sofía, a move which the family opposed.

As far as the permanent collection at the Reina Sofía is concerned, it was officially inaugurated by King Juan Carlos and Queen Sofía in September 1992. The museum houses works derived from a number of sources, including the Museo Español de Arte Contemporáneo and the Museo del Prado. The diverse collection spans the period between the end of the 19th century and the present day, grouped according to movements.

The "Cubism – Early Avant-Garde" section features works by Picasso, Juan Gris, Braque and Léger, amongst others. The section entitled "Picasso – The Context of *Guernica*" features a selection of work by Picasso from this period, as well as works by other artists who appeared at the 1937 Paris Exhibition – such as Alexander Calder and Joan Miró – and photographs by Robert Capa. The Surrealists are represented by Dalí, Miró, Max Ernst, Magritte, Man Ray and Brassaï, to name just the best known.

One particular gallery focuses on artists who have played key roles in the development of Spanish art, such as Saura, Chillida and Arroyo. Modern international art is represented by a limited selection of works from the likes of Mark Rothko, Francis Bacon, Cy Twombly and Henry Moore.

Above: Museo Nacional Reina Sofía; **right:** People walking past the towering glass lift that makes the Museo Nacional Reina Sofía instantly recognisable

Museo Thyssen-Bornemisza

This splendid museum is one of the three points on what is known as Madrid's Golden Triangle of Art, together with the Prado and the Reina Sofía Museums. It houses one of the most important art collections in the world – the private collection of the late Baron Hans Heinrich Thyssen-Bornemisza.

It was his father, Baron Heinrich Thyssen-Bornemisza, who started the collection in the 1920s. Baron Heinrich bought the Villa Favorita in Lugano, Switzerland, from Prince Leopold of Prussia to house it. When he died, the collection was divided up amongst his heirs. His youngest son, Hans Heinrich, inherited his title and also bought back the works from his various family members.

In the 1960s, Hans Heinrich began to expand and develop his collection with modern art acquisitions, including pieces

by the German Expressionists. As a result of this, larger premises were required and several countries showed interest in acquiring the paintings.

The collection first toured to Madrid on a nine-year loan, where it has been on display since 1992. In 1993, the Spanish government provided the finance for the Thyssen-Bornemisza Museum to acquire the collection on a permanent basis. No doubt the Baron's wife – Carmen "Tita" Cervera, a former Miss Spain – was influential in the decision to bring it to Spain.

Above left: Outside of the museum, with the new Cervera wing at right angles; **above right:** Visitors entering the museum

✚ **61 E2**

✉ **Museo Thyssen-Bornemisza**
Paseo del Prado 8

☎ 91 369 0151

🔳 **www.museothyssen.org**

🕐 Tue–Sun 10–7, 24 and 31 Dec 10–3, closed 1 Jan and 1 May

✋ Inexpensive

🚇 Banco de España

Above left: The entrance hall of the Thyssen-Bornemisza Museum; **above centre:** The museum stages many temporary exhibitions, often introducing new styles and artists to the public

The collection had been housed at first (since its arrival here in 1992) in the neo-classical Palacio de Villahermosa, an early 19th-century edifice that was restored by the Spanish architect Rafael Moneo, something of an expert in grand revamps. New features included terracotta walls, marble floors and skylights that provided optimum illumination in which to view the works. A new wing was inaugurated in June 2004, exhibiting paintings from Carmen Cervera's own collection.

The two collections amount to almost 1,000 works that span the history of Western art from the 13th century to the end of the 20th century. These complement the collections housed at the Prado and the Reina Sofía, and feature a wide variety of movements – Italian and Dutch primitives, 17th-century Dutch paintings, Impressionism, German Expressionism, Russian Constructivism, geometric abstraction and pop art.

Indeed, the museum contains several masterpieces. Probably the most famous painting is Domenico Ghirlandaio's idealised

portrait of Giovanna Tornabuoni. Old masters of note include works by Duccio, Jan van Eyck and Petrus Christus. The 16th-century and baroque periods are represented by Titian, Caravaggio, Rubens and Tintoretto, for example, whilst the Impressionists include Monet, Manet, Renoir, Cézanne and Degas. Several rooms are set aside for the German Expressionists, with works by Nolde, Macke, Kirchner, Marc, Dix and Russian Kandinsky, who formed the abstract Blaue Reiter group.

The modern masters include paintings by Braque, Mondrian, Klee, Max Ernst and Picasso. Finally a few rooms feature works by modern American artists such as Georgia O'Keeffe, Hopper and Rauschenberg.

Carmen Cervera's collection consists of over 600 works, including paintings by Brueghel the Elder, Canaletto and Guardi amongst the old masters. The 19th and early 20th-century is mainly represented through works by Corot, Monet, Sisley, Renoir, Degas, Gauguin, Picasso, Braque, Matisse, Gris, Nolde and Kandinsky, amongst others. There is also a Rodin room containing four sculptures by the legendary French artist.

Above right: *Thank You*, by Richard Lindner (1971) from the gallery's Surrealist, and pop art collection

Plaza de Cascorro

This small, triangular plaza is the *tapón*, or lid, of the Rastro flea market. It has undergone several name changes over the years – including Plazuela del Rastro and, in 1913, Plaza de Nicolás Salmerón. Colloquially, it became known as the Plaza de Cascorro at the start of the 20th century, with reference to the statue of the hero of the Spanish–Cuban War, Eloy Gonzalo – indeed, it is the square's centrepiece.

According to legend, in September 1896, Gonzalo volunteered to ignite a camp in the town of Cascorro, which housed several thousand Cuban rebels. His one-man mission was a success, but he died in a military hospital several months later.

The name for this square has stuck and was made official in 1941. The 2.3m (7.55-foot) bronze statue in the middle of the plaza is the work of Aniceto Marinas and depicts the valiant Gonzalo – rifle slung over one shoulder, a torch in one hand and a can of petrol in the other. It was unveiled by King Alfonso XIII on 5 May 1902.

Today the plaza only really comes to life on Sundays, when the Rastro gets into full swing.

Plaza de la Cebada

The area known as the Plaza de la Cebada grew out of several plots of barren land just outside the city wall. It gained its name from a legumes and grain market that sprang up here during the 16th century.

It was from here that *cebada*, separated barley, would be obtained for the horses of the king's cavalry.

During the 19th century, executions were carried out here – including those of the Spanish general Rafael del Riego and highwayman Luis Candelas.

In 1870, in response to a public health and safety report, King Alfonso XII ordered a market to be built in the area. A huge cast-iron and glass structure, designed by Mariano Calvo Pereira and modelled on Victor Baltard's Les Halles market (then recently completed) in Paris. The market of the Plaza de la Cebada was inaugurated on 11 June, 1875.

However, that original building was demolished in 1956 and replaced by the current structure of steel and prefabricated concrete. The area is due another facelift in the coming years: the market and sports centre are to be bulldozed and replaced.

The many cafés and bars surrounding the market make it a popular location for open-air drinks and tapas, particularly on Sundays after the Rastro.

Plaza del Conde de Barajas

This square is a veritable haven of tranquillity after the hustle and bustle of the adjacent Plaza Mayor, though on Sundays it becomes an impromptu open-air art gallery featuring local artists.

If you walk down the stone steps under the Arco de Cuchilleros in the southwest corner of the Plaza Mayor, you will have

Left: The market of Plaza de la Cebada; **above:** Plaza del Conde de Barajas

passed one of Madrid's oldest taverns – Las Cuevas de Luis Candelas. This is on the corner of Cava Baja and San Miguel, bordered by the sloping outside wall of the Plaza Mayor, which contains a number of popular *mesónes* or taverns.

However, if you turn right after Luis Candelas, you will encounter the quiet Plaza del Conde de Barajas. The tranquillity here is only broken by the sound of people enjoying their food and drink on the one café terrace belonging to the restaurant of the same name, the Conde de Barajas, which also doubles up as a piano bar.

The square takes on a totally different character on Sundays from noon to 2pm, however, when there is a chance for passers-by to view paintings by 30 artists.

Plaza de las Cortes

Two of the most striking buildings in the Plaza de las Cortes are the Westin Palace Hotel and the Congreso de los Diputados, or Parliament Building. These two are separated by the Carrera San Jerónimo, which links Plaza de Neptuno to the Puerta del Sol.

The Congreso de los Diputados was built in the mid-19th century, on the site of a disused monastery. It is an imposing building with Corinthian columns and sculpted pediments. Huge bronze lions grace its steps. It is perhaps best known as the place where the Civil Guard, led by Lieutenant-Colonel Tejero, attempted a military coup in 1981. During the coup attempt, press reporters from the world over took up position across the road, in the Westin Palace Hotel.

Favoured by statesmen and celebrities alike, the Westin Palace Hotel is one of the most elegant hotels in Madrid.

Below: Congreso de los Diputados

Plaza de Cascorro

✚ **61 C3**

✉ **Plaza de Cascorro**

Ⓜ La Latina or Tirso de Molina

Plaza de la Cebada

✚ **61 C3**

✉ **Plaza de la Cebada**

Ⓜ La Latina

Plaza del Conde de Barajas

✚ **61 C2**

✉ **Plaza del Conde de Barajas**

Ⓜ Tirso de Molina or La Latina

Plaza de las Cortes

✚ **61 E2**

✉ **Plaza de las Cortes**

Ⓜ Banco de España

Plaza Mayor

In the 15th century, what occupied this space was a simple market square, known as the Plaza del Arrabal (*arrabal* indicating the poor areas), containing slum dwellings. The Plaza Mayor that we know today is a spectacular 17th-century square complete with steep grey slate roofs, dormer windows and spiky pinnacles.

Once Madrid acquired the status of capital city in 1561, Juan de Herrera was commissioned by Philip II to renovate the square. He was also the designer of El Escorial, Philip II's austere palace some 50km (31 miles) from Madrid. However, the only section of the plaza to be built at that point was the Casa de la Panadería (the

bakers' guild). Little progress was made until 1617, when Juan Gómez de Mora – Herrera's successor – continued with the project and had the square built within a two-year period.

The oldest part of the square is thus the Casa de la Panadería, which is also the most ornate building here. It is located

on the north side of the square. Originally constructed on granite supports, the Bakers' Guild provided a thoroughfare to Calle Mayor. Unfortunately, most of the building was destroyed by fire in 1672, with only the portal surviving. The façade, which was restored, is now decorated with allegorical paintings.

The south side of the Plaza Mayor contains the Casa de la Carnicería, where meat was once sold. It now houses some municipal buildings. Another emblematic feature of the Plaza Mayor is a spectacular

flight of stone steps linking the Arco de Cuchilleros (see page 62) in the southwest corner to the Calle de Cuchilleros, where knife-grinders had their workshops and which is today lined with mesónes or taverns.

The centre of the square is graced by a 1616 bronze statue of Philip III on

Above left: Phillip III on horseback in front of the Casa de la Panadería; **above right:** Walking beneath the cool cloisters of Casa de la Panadería

✚ **61 C2**

✉ **Plaza Mayor**
Plaza Mayor

🚇 Sol

horseback by Giambologna and Pietro Tacca, which was moved to the Plaza Mayor from the Casa de Campo in the 19th century.

The Plaza Mayor was originally designed for ceremonies and public events. The first to be held here was a ceremony in 1620 in honour of San Isidro, the patron saint of Madrid, who had been beatified two years previously. Later it became the scene of executions, bullfights, autos-da-fé (public penances) and performances of all kinds.

The tradition of performance in the Plaza Mayor continues to this present day. The square provides an ideal outside location for concerts, particularly during the San Isidro festivities in mid-May. This is also the venue for a stamp and coin market on Sunday mornings, as well as for a popular Christmas market selling Christmas trees and tacky decorations throughout December.

The Plaza Mayor also provides an ideal setting in which to contemplate the magnificent architecture, over a meal or a drink on one of the numerous attractive, albeit expensive, café terraces that line the square.

Above: People taking a break from sightseeing at one of the numerous attractive cafés that line Plaza Mayor

Plaza de la Paja

Today, Plaza de la Paja is a quiet, pretty square nestling in the heart of old Madrid. In its early days, it must have been bustling with activity, for the labyrinth of streets and squares between Calle de la Morería, Plaza de la Paja and Puerta de Moros formed the Morería (the Moorish quarter).

In medieval times, the Plaza de la Paja (Straw Square), was the corn and fodder market. Peasants who laboured on the land by the river had to donate a percentage of their crop to the church. Hence the square was often teeming with crowds of people and was always covered in straw. At the same time, wealthy families took up residence in houses surrounding the square. This is where the Mudéjar Muslim community lived for over four centuries.

Among the few buildings that survived reconstruction in the Plaza de la Paja in the 19th century are the Iglesia de San Andrés, with its cherub-covered dome. Sadly, the only remaining feature of the original structure of San Andrés is the bell tower, as the church suffered serious damage following a fire in 1936, at the beginning of the Civil War. Other survivors of the reconstruction include the Capilla del Obispo and Capilla de San Isidro.

The history of the Plaza de la Paja is closely linked to that of San Isidro, the patron saint of Madrid, and his employers, the Vargas family. Isidro was a peasant who performed miracles. When he died, he was buried in a pauper's grave and his remains were kept in the Iglesia de San Andrés. Later, the Vargas family built a chapel to house his remains, the Capilla del Obispo – but it was never used. However, when Isidro was canonised in the 17th century, the Capilla de San Isidro was built, and is one of the few examples of Gothic architecture in Madrid to have remained intact.

Left: The large slate cupola of the church of San Andrés, which stands at the top end of Madrid's Plaza de la Paja, topped with a lantern and decorated with statues set into the surrounding niches

🚇 **61 C3**

✉ **Plaza de la Paja**
Plaza de la Paja

Ⓜ La Latina

Plaza de Santa Ana

This must be one of Madrid's liveliest squares, taking its name from the 16th-century convent that stood here previously. It was created by Napoleon Bonaparte's brother, Joseph, who ruled from 1805 to 1812. He demolished many religious edifices to make way for squares such as the Plaza de Oriente and Plaza de Santa Ana. Indeed, Joseph became known as El Rey de las Plazuelas (the king of the squares).

The Plaze de Santa Ana was also the site of the Corral del Príncipe, a 16th-century theatre where Golden Age plays were performed. In 1745, the Corral was replaced by the Teatro del Príncipe. The Café del Príncipe, popular with artists and writers, was situated just to the right of the theatre. The theatre was renovated in the 19th century and became the Teatro Español (under renovation until 2010). The façade was reconstructed at a later date. Today it displays the busts of Golden Age playwrights such as Calderón de la Barca and Tirso de Molina. Busts of key 20th-century playwrights, including García Lorca and Valle-Inclán, grace the more modern section of the façade.

The square also features two statues with theatrical links: a statue of Calderón de la Barca commemorates one of Spain's leading Golden Age playwrights; the playwright and poet Federico García Lorca also reappears in statue form – his was erected in 1998 to celebrate the centenary of his birth. Both face the Teatro Español. The former stands in front of the spectacular hotel ME, which used to be popular with bullfighters who fought at the Ventas bullring.

Numerous bars and restaurants line the other two sides of the square, including the popular Cervecería Alemana, which was frequented by celebrities such as Ernest Hemingway and bullfighters "Manolete" and Luis Miguel Dominguín.

Below: Detail of the façade of the Casa de Guadalajara on the Plaza de Santa Ana, with a painting of a castle surrounded by gardens made up of a large set of tiles

61 D2

Plaza de Santa Ana
Plaza de Santa Ana

Sol or Sevilla

Plaza de la Villa

This is Madrid's oldest square. Originally an Arab souk, it was in fact the city's main marketplace in both Muslim and early medieval times, until the Plaza Mayor was constructed in the 17th century. The Plaza de la Villa comprises three distinguished buildings, each featuring a different architectural style.

The oldest building in the square is the early 15th-century Casa y Torre de los Lujanes, which was once the residence of the powerful Lujanes family. The Casa was restored in the 1920s, in the *aparejo toledano* style, using a combination of brick, flint and mortar. The right side of the building features a Mudéjar door and a carved stone balustrade; on the left there is a Gothic portal. It is believed that Francois I of France was imprisoned in the tower by Charles V after the Battle of Pavia in 1525.

Opposite the Casa de los Lujanes is the Casa de la Villa – the City Hall, which

it was until very recently. The building was designed by Juan Gómez de Mora in 1630 – the architect who completed the Plaza Mayor – and it dominates the square. It boasts similar architectural features to the Plaza Mayor, with its slanting roofs with dormer windows and the spires at the corners. The Casa de la Villa was not completed until 1695, due to financial problems. A century later, in the late 1780s, Juan de Villanueva, the architect of the Prado Museum, added a balcony that would enable the royal family to watch the Corpus Christi processions. There are guided tours on Mondays at 5pm.

The third building in the Plaza de la Villa is the Casa de Cisneros, with its striking Plateresque façade. The house was built in 1537 as a palace for a relative of Cardenal Cisneros, the founder of the University of Alcalá. The building was restored in 1910 and now houses municipal offices.

Above: Casa de los Lujanes

✚ **61 C2**

✉ **Plaza de la Villa**
Plaza de la Villa

🚇 Opera

Puerta del Sol

This square originally started life as the eastern gate of 15th-century Madrid. The gateway was pulled down in 16th century, at which point the area became a square bordered by the Hospital del Buen Suceso and the convents of Nuestra Señora de la Victoria and San Felipe el Real.

The steps and cloister of the San Felipe el Real became the venue for a gossip, or *mentidero*. Such was the importance of this social phenomenon that *mentideros* regularly featured in the works of Golden Age writers such as Lope de Vega and Cervantes. The square was renovated in the 19th century and the *mentidero* venues were replaced by cafés. One of the most famous of these was the Café Pombo, on the corner of Calle Carretas, nowadays a fashion store.

The Casa de Correos is the most imposing building in the square. It was originally designed by Jaime Marquet in the 1760s, to be a post office during Charles III's reign. In 1847, it became the headquarters for the ministry of the interior. Another 19 years later, the clock tower was built. During the Franco regime, abuses of human rights were reported to have taken place in the police cells located in the basement of the building. Today the Casa de Correos is the headquarters

of the Madrid regional government, the Comunidad de Madrid.

The Sol square itself has been the scene of numerous events over the centuries. For example, there was rioting in 1766 against the Marqués de Squillace (Esquilache), who tried to prohibit the wearing of long capes and wide-brimmed hats on the pretext that

Left: A statue depicting Charles III astride his horse overlooks Puerta del Sol; **above:** The semicircular paving stone known as "Kilómetro Cero", which marks the centre of Spain from which all distances are measured, on Puerta del Sol

✚ **61 D2**

✉ **Puerta del Sol**
Puerta del Sol

🚇 Sol

criminals could not only conceal their ill-gotten gains thus, but also their identity. On 2 May, 1808, a crowd of Madrileños were charged by Napoleon's cavalry, the "Mamelukes", here in the Sol square: this scene is depicted in Goya's painting *Dos de Mayo*, or *The 2nd of May*. In 1912, Prime Minister Canalejas was assassinated in Sol. In 1931, the Second Republic was declared from a balcony outside the interior-ministry offices.

The Sol of the present day is still the scene of demonstrations and meetings. Thousands of people gather here on New Year's Eve, under the clock tower. When the clock strikes midnight, everyone eats 12 grapes, in time with the 12 chimes of the clock. Sol is also a popular meeting place. People tend to gather near one of of Sol's

two most emblematic features: the plaque for the Kilómetro Cero and the statue of a bear under a *madroño* tree (*Arbutus menziesii*, the strawberry tree).

The Kilómetro Cero is placed on the ground outside the Casa de Correos – it is from this spot that all distances in Spain are measured. The bear and madroño, standing on the corner of Calle del Carmen, constitute the symbol of Madrid – it also appears on the badge of Atlético de Madrid, the city's "other" main football team. Another emblematic feature of Sol has to be the Tío Pepe sign dominating the square from its position on the roof of the Hotel Paris.

Above: The Bear and Tree statue in Puerta del Sol

El Rastro

This is Madrid's most famous flea market. Locals and tourists alike gravitate to the Rastro in droves every Sunday, all year round. The days when bargains could be found are no more and you have to look hard before you can spot a worthy buy but this is still a great place to come at the weekend.

61 C4

El Rastro
Calle de la Ribera de Curtidores

La Latina, Tirso de Molina or Embajadores

Above: The bustling flea market at the Rastro

The market area itself is bordered by the San Millán, Embajadores and Toledo streets, with the main drag starting at Plaza de Cascorro and running down Ribera de Curtidores. Most vendors start setting up their stalls around 8:30 in the morning and trade typically starts winding down around 2:30 in the afternoon. Almost 1,700 stalls sell a considerable variety of goods – plants, clothes, household goods, bric-a-brac, magazines, books and ceramics. There are several antiques specialists, in particular in the Galerías Piquer at Ribera de Curtidores 29; but the items here tend to be on the pricey side.

Off to the west, at the bottom end of the Rastro, is the Plaza del Campillo del Mundo Nuevo, a large open area where you might still find some people selling old car parts, assorted junk, collections of old magazines (many of them pornographic) and comics. Much of the stuff on sale here may be of little real interest to the shopper. The point is, however, that the Rastro isn't really that much about shopping – for many, it is simply an excuse to meet up with friends and hop between the numerous bars in the area, sampling tapas, usually washed down with a cold beer or a glass of vermouth.

The origins of the Rastro are vague. The earliest mention of a market in this area dates from around the 15th century. Later references appear in the literary works of Carlos Arniches, Ricardo de la Vega and Ramón Gómez de la Serna.

"El rastro" refers to the smears of blood left as animal carcasses were dragged up the hill from the slaughterhouses on Ronda de Valencia to the tanneries near Plaza de Cascorro. The tanneries and slaughterhouse have long disappeared; but other historical places of interest remain. For example, the iconic statue of Eloy Gonzalo, can of petrol in hand, standing in the centre of Plaza de Cascorro is a reminder of Spain's involvement in the Spanish–Cuban war. At the top of Calle Carlos Arniches, the former Corralón – an early 19th-century tenement block – has become the Museo de Artes y Tradiciones Populares, a museum dedicated to the plastic arts such as ceramics, basketry, glassware and iron work.

Above: An array of magazines at the Rastro flea market; **right:** Curios for sale

Real Academia de Bellas Artes de San Fernando

This is actually the city's oldest permanent artistic institution. The Real Academia de Bellas Artes de San Fernando (San Fernando Royal Academy of Fine Arts) is located in the very heart of Madrid, on Calle de Alcalá, next to the bustling Puerta del Sol.

It is housed in a palace that was built by José Benito de Churriguera in 1725 and later acquired for the newly established Academia de Bellas Artes. At this point, Diego de Villanueva was commissioned to modernise the building and he made

Left: Portrait of the Marchioness of Llano by Anton Raphael Mengs; **above:** The façade of Real Academia de Bellas Artes de San Fernando

✚ **61 E2**

✉ **Real Academia de Bellas Artes de San Fernando**
Calle de Alcalá 13

☎ 91 524 0864

🌐 http://rabasf.insde.es

🕐 Tue–Fri 9–7, Sat 9–2:30, 4–7, Sun and public hols 9–2:30

✋ Inexpensive

🚇 Sol or Sevilla

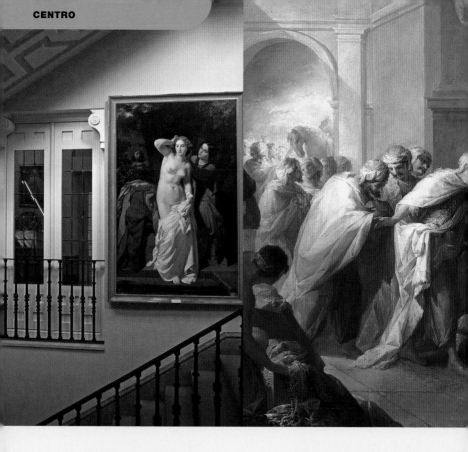

Above left: The interior of Real Academia de Bellas Artes de San Fernando; **above centre:** A painting depicting a Catholic king and queen receiving a Moorish ambassador

important changes to the façade. Over 200 years later – in the 1980s, under the auspices of Fernando Chueca – further renovation of the building took place. The aim was to display the academy's extensive collection of works of art, which is doubtless one of the most important in Spain.

There are over 1,000 paintings and sculptures on show, spanning four centuries, from the 16th to the 20th. However, despite the size of the collection,

the Real Academia receives relatively few visitors in comparison with the "big three" museums that make up the Golden Triangle of Art – the Prado, the Thyssen and the Reina Sofía.

The museum's main attractions include 13 works by Goya, a former director of the academy when it was first established. The works include two major self-portraits as well as *El Entierro de la Sardina* (the burial of the sardine) – a carnival scene that perhaps serves as a prelude to his later dark works – and a large portrait of Godoy, an unpopular minister under Charles III. Works by other important Spanish artists from the 16th to the 19th centuries are also exhibited, among them Ribera, Murillo,

El Greco and Velázquez. A highlight is Zurbarán's *Fray Pedro Machado*.

As far as foreign artists are concerned, one of the Real Academia de Bellas Artes' key possessions is the Italian mannerist Giuseppe Arcimboldo's *Spring*. Arcimboldo was the official portrait painter at the imperial court of Austria in the mid-16th century. In 1563, he painted portraits of the four seasons for Ferdinand I of Austria. The portraits are made up of objects that represent those seasons. Hence *Spring* is a surrealistic portrait of a man, entirely composed of flowers. Arcimboldo was viewed by many Surrealists as the "father of Surrealism". Works by Raphael, Titian, Rubens and van Dyck are also on show.

Apart from paintings, the Real Academia de Bellas Artes boasts an important collection of rare books, plans and sketches – including a set of drawings by Juan de Villanueva, who designed the Prado Museum. This Calcografía Nacional (the national collection of engravings) is found in the same building. It contains an important archive of prints and engravings, including the original plates for Goya's series of etchings and a number of engravings by Picasso, who was a former student of the academy (as was Salvador Dalí).

Above right: A portrait of Mariana of Austria, Queen of Spain

San Pedro el Viejo

Probably built on the site of a mosque, San Pedro el Viejo is certainly one of the oldest churches in Madrid. It was originally located near Puerta Cerrada near the Plaza Mayor, and moved to its present-day site in Calle del Nuncio in 1345, during the reign of Alfonso XI.

Originally named San Pedro el Real, the most striking features of the church are its 14th-century Mudéjar-style brick tower, iron-framed arched windows and striking Renaissance-style west portal from 1525. Its south portal boasts a royal coat of arms that dates from before the reign of Ferdinand and Isabella – it is the only one of its kind to survive in the capital. However, much of San Pedro el Viejo dates from the 17th century, when it underwent renovation

work under the auspices of the Archbishop of Brindisi, Lorenzo Reinoso and the architect Francisco Sanz.

Inside, San Pedro el Viejo houses an effigy of *Jesús el Pobre* (Jesus the Poor), which is one of the highlights of the Semana Santa (Easter) processions.

It also contains a painting of one of Madrid's favourite female patron saints, *La Virgen de la Paloma*, which hangs above the altar. Legend has it that a man

who was collecting wood near the church accidentally came across the painting. However, he was more interested in the frame than the actual painting, as he could use it for firewood. He gave the painting to some children, one of whom was related to a certain Isabel Tintero, who had the painting restored and placed by the entrance to her house on Calle de la Paloma. Tintero's sister-in-law then had her newborn child blessed before this painting of the Virgin. After this, such was the interest in the Virgin that Tintero had

to free up a section of her house to make room for the numerous visitors. A chapel was later built for the Virgin; but in the end, the painting was moved to the church of San Pedro el Real, where it still hangs to this day.

✝ **61 C3**

✉ **San Pedro el Viejo**
Costanilla de San Pedro

☎ 91 365 1284

🕐 Daily 8–12:30, 5–8

Ⓜ La Latina

Above left and right: San Pedro el Viejo, one of the oldest churches in Madrid, flanked by apartments

Jerónimos and the East

There are many splendid sights in this part of Madrid, dating from various epochs. But it is hard to avoid the temptation to attribute the feel of the area principally to one man: Charles III (1716–88). On succeeding his half-brother Fernando VI in 1759, this enlightened despot was unimpressed with the capital city he had inherited and set about improving it energetically, becoming known as Madrid's "Alcalde Rey" (mayor king). He it was who set in motion a series of projects that would embellish the city considerably, most notably the Puerta de Alcalá, the Salón (now Paseo) del Prado, the Prado Museum and the Botanical Gardens.

CARLETON PLACE
PUBLIC LIBRARY

JERÓNIMOS AND THE EAST WALK

1. Estación de Atocha See page 105
Begin at this great example of a revitalised public space. Built between 1888 and 1892, in the classic 19th-century style of wrought iron and glass, Atocha station was a century later dirty and dilapidated – until being spectacularly revamped by the architect Rafael Moneo and turned into a tropical garden. Whole new sections were built for the inauguration of the high-speed AVE service in 1992.

2. Museo del Prado See page 108
From Atocha, head west along Avenida de la Ciudad de Barcelona and walk up the Paseo del Prado past the Real Jardín Botánico, worth a visit in itself, to Museo del Prado. You will need more than a brief visit to do the Prado justice. However, if time is short, do not miss the rooms showing works by Goya, Velázquez or El Greco, or those dedicated to the 16th- and 17th-century Spanish painting.

3. Parque del Retiro See page 113
From the Prado, head east up Calle de Felipe IV, past the Real Academia Española and the Casón del Buen Retiro (an annexe of the Prado). Cross Calle Alfonso XII into the park. The Retiro is an invitation to laze around, but make time to find the statue of the *Fallen Angel* and the exhibition spaces of the Palacio de Cristal and the Palacio de Velázquez.

4. Puerta de Alcalá See page 119
Make your way to the northwest corner of the Parque del Retiro. Just outside is one of Madrid's most emblematic monuments – the huge, five-arch Puerta de Alcalá, created by Palermo-born Francesco Sabatini, court architect to Charles III. This gate is a reminder that Madrid remained a walled city until the 1860s. Sabatini presented Charles with two plans and he wanted *both* – look carefully at each side to spot the differences!

5. Plaza de Cibeles See page 116
Heading west down Calle de Alcalá, you reach one of the most important junctions in central Madrid, Plaza de Cibeles. In the middle is the monument and fountain depicting Cybele, a Phrygian goddess, in her lion-drawn chariot. Real Madrid fans regularly celebrate their team's victories here. Notice another important building bordering the square: the Palacio de Comunicaciones, formerly the post office.

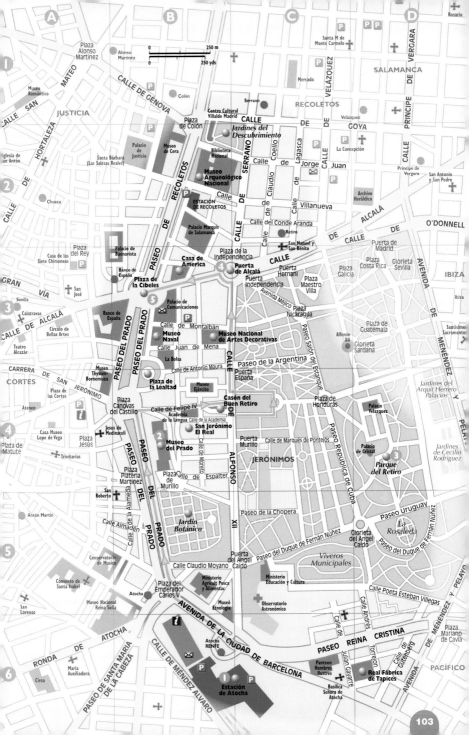

Casa de América

This cultural centre hosts a great many activities with a focus on the arts in Latin America. It is housed in the beautiful Palacio de Linares, built in 1873 for the Marqués of Linares by the architect Carlos Colubí.

It is worth taking one of the guided tours to the see the exquisite interior, which includes a rich selection of furnishings, lamps and bronzes from Paris, many works of art and a fabulous white marble staircase as well as, if you believe in these things, a ghost.

Artists, both well-known figures and emerging talents, are frequently showcased in the many art exhibitions held throughout the year. There are also regular film and theatre seasons, concerts, and talks by leading writers, film directors, playwrights, intellectuals and political figures. At any time of year, therefore, it is worth checking out the programme to see what's on.

In addition to whatever's current, there is a bookshop, print and video libraries for academics, and a fine terrace restaurant where visitors can enjoy open-air arts events on balmy summer evenings.

Cason del Buen Retiro

One of only two surviving buildings from the Palacio del Buen Retiro, originally built by the Conde-Duque de Olivares for King Philip IV in the 1630s, the Casón was once its ballroom. Now an annexe of the Museo del Prado, it was reopened to the public early in 2008 after a decade of extensive renovation work.

The main floor of the Casón del Buen Retiro is used for temporary exhibitions complementing those held in the Prado, while the others house archives, a library, a reading room, a meeting room and an educational centre. The top floor is earmarked as the home of the conservation department.

One of the achievements of the remodelling project was the recuperation of the fresco in the central vault, painted by Luca Giordano in 1697, which represents the *Allegory of the Golden Fleece*, in homage to the Spanish monarchy. To mark the Casón's reopening, there was an exhibition of 75 of Giordano's drawings, water colours, oil paintings and engravings.

Several such excellent showings are scheduled, so visitors should keep an eye on the Prado website for information.

Below: The neo baroque Casa de América cultural centre which showcases Latin-American art

Above: The Casón del Buen Retiro, the only reminder of Buen Retiro Palace dating from the 17th century

Estación de Atocha

Atocha station is a great example of the successful revitalisation of a run-down public space. Built between 1888 and 1892 in wrought iron and glass, in classic 19th-century style, Atocha was dirty and dilapidated by the 1980s.

Madrid's year as the European City of Culture in 1992 was a good excuse to spruce up the city. It also coincided with the Sevilla Expo, for which Spain's first high-speed rail link, the AVE, was built.

In order to make room for the new trains, a completely new station was built further out, while the old station was converted into a concourse including shops, cafés and a 4,000sq m (4785sq yards) covered tropical garden. The shopping complex never really took off, but the tropical garden is a pleasant place to sit and people-watch. In the nearby commuter station, there is a moving monument to the victims of the vicious terrorist attack on 11 March, 2004. On that fateful day, 10 backpack bombs placed in several commuter trains exploded in four different locations during the morning rush hour, killing 191 and injuring hundreds more.

Above: The indoor palm garden at Estación de Atocha

Casa de América

✚ 103 B3

✉ **Casa de América**
Plaza de Cibeles 2

☎ 91 595 4800

🌐 www.casamerica.es

🕐 Exhibitions Mon–Sat 11–8, Sat–Sun 11–3. Building, guided visits only Sat–Sun every half hour 10–2

✋ Free, guided tours expensive

🚇 Banco de España

Casón del Buen Retiro

✚ 103 B4

✉ **Casón del Buen Retiro**
Calle Alfonso XII 28

☎ 91 330 2800 (through the Museo del Prado switchboard)

🌐 www.museodelprado.es

🕐 Wed–Sun noon–8

✋ Inexpensive

🚇 Atocha or Banco de España

Estación de Atocha

✚ 103 B6

✉ **Estación de Atocha**
Glorieta del Emperador Carlos V

☎ 91 527 4627

✋ Free

🚇 Atocha or Atocha Renfe

Jardines del Descubrimiento

Essentially a part of the Plaza de Colón – of which they take up the whole of the eastern flank – these Gardens of the Discovery celebrate the discovery of America. They were inaugurated in 1970.

The southwestern corner of the lovely Gardens is presided over by the tall monument to Columbus. The eastern side has four enormous concrete blocks that are adorned with carved drawings and texts alluding to Columbus' journey to the New World.

The theatre on the gardens' western edge was renamed in honour of the actor, writer and director Fernando Fernán Gómez, who died in November 2007.

Museo Arqueológico Nacional

Sharing the same enormous building as the Biblioteca Nacional (National Library), Madrid's archaeological museum is one of the city's oldest, dating from 1867.

The collections trace the history of human cultures from prehistoric times until the 15th century. There are artefacts from Iberian, Celtic, Greek, Egyptian, Punic, Roman, Paleochristian, Visigothic and Muslim cultures, a great many of them from digs carried out in Spain itself.

The museum's prized possession is the *Dama de Elche*, a stone bust of an Iberian priestess reckoned to be from 500 BC. Another major attraction is the reproduction of the cave paintings found at Altamira, which is in a vault in the museum's garden.

Jardines del Descubrimiento

✚ 103 B2

✉ **Jardines del Descubrimiento**
Bounded by Plaza de Colón, Calle Goya, Calle Serrano, Calle Jorge Juan

🕐 Open daily 24 hours

✋ Free

Ⓜ Colón or Serrano

Museo Arqueológico Nacional

✚ 103 B2

✉ **Museo Arqueológico Nacional**
Calle Serrano 13

☎ 91 577 7912

🌐 http://man.mcu.es

🕐 Tue–Sat 9:30–8, Sun and public hols 9:30–3

✋ Inexpensive, free during renovation work

Ⓜ Serrano

Below: The monument to Columbus constructed in the late 19th century

Museo Nacional de Artes Decorativas

Located in a small palace that was formerly the home of the Duquesa de Santoña, Spain's national museum for the decorative arts was one of the first museums of its kind in Europe.

This fascinating museum holds a collection of over 40,000 objets d'art, glassware, porcelain, tapestries and furniture, some 15,000 of which are on show permanently. The collection is mainly composed of items from Spain, but there is also an important selection of pieces from China.

Of great interest is the exhibit of an 18th-century tiled kitchen, transferred piece by piece from a Valencian mansion. The 1,604 hand-painted wall tiles wrapping it show a detailed domestic scene – a sort of kitchen with a kitchen, right down to servants making hot chocolate in the background!

Museo Naval

Of great interest for all those interested in Spain's maritime history, this naval museum shows – in a slightly chaotic if chronological fashion – a great many pieces of the booty acquired by Columbus and other mariners during Spain's period of naval and colonial expansion.

As well as these, there are examples of navigational aids, weaponry of all types, models of ships and an array of maps and wall charts of various eras. The most important among the latter is the first known map of the Americas to be made by a European – Juan de la Cosa's parchment drawing made, it is believed, for Ferdinand and Isabella around 1500.

Above: Mosaic with fish designs at Museo Arqueológico Nacional

---

Museo Nacional de Artes Decorativas

➕ **103 B3**

✉ **Museo Nacional de Artes Decorativas**
Calle Montalbán, 12

☎ 91 532 6499

🌐 **http://mnartesdecorativas.mcu.es**

🕐 Tue–Wed and Fri–Sat 9:30–3, Thu 9:30–3 and 5–8, Sun and public hols 10–3

✋ Inexpensive, free Sun

🚇 Banco de España or Retiro

Museo Naval

➕ **103 B3**

✉ **Museo Naval**
Paseo del Prado 5

☎ 91 523 8789

🌐 **www.museonavalmadrid.com**

🕐 Tue–Sun 10–2; closed 1 Jan, Maundy (Holy) Thursday and Good Friday, 1 and 15 May, 16 Jul, 1–31 Aug, 9 Nov, and 24–25 and 31 Dec

✋ Free

🚇 Banco de España

Museo del Prado

Undoubtedly Madrid's greatest attraction, the Prado Museum brought visitors to the city even before the age of mass tourism and budget air travel. It is one of the world's truly great art palaces.

The Museo del Prado houses a vast collection of paintings, sculptures, prints, drawings and other valuable pieces, of which fewer than 10 per cent – some 1,300 works – are actually on show. Even this is far too many to do justice to during one visit – or in this book – so anyone seriously interested in exploring it fully should consider returning. For those short of time, the museum recommends itineraries of the not-to-be-missed highlights in its collection.

The Prado has undergone lengthy – and costly – expansion and modernisation in recent years, meaning much more space is now available for showing works previously held in storage, as well as for more temporary exhibitions.

A whole new wing was inaugurated in late 2007. Rafael Moneo's elegant and sober cube-shaped brick building stands on the site of the ruins of a cloister, next to the San Jerónimos church. The

cube actually includes the original stone "skeleton" of the former cloisters as part of its interior architecture – the almost 2,800 stone blocks were dismantled, restored and then reassembled inside the new building. The wing provides enough exhibition space for 400 works to be displayed as well as the space for restoration, picture storage, an auditorium, a bookshop and a restaurant.

Another important project was the renovation and expansion of the Casón del Buen Retiro annexe (see page 104), reopened early in 2008. Eventually the Prado's expansion will be completed by absorbing the nearby Palacio del Buen Retiro, which currently houses the Army Museum.

Above left: Interior of Museo del Prado; **above right:** Detail of the Goya Statue

✚ **103 B4**

✉ **Museo del Prado**
Paseo del Prado s/n

☎ 91 330 2800

🌐 **www.museodelprado.es**

🕐 Tue–Sun 9–8 (24 and 31 Dec and 6 Jan 9–2)

✋ Moderate, free from 6pm daily (5pm Sun) and for under-18s

🚇 Banco de España or Atocha

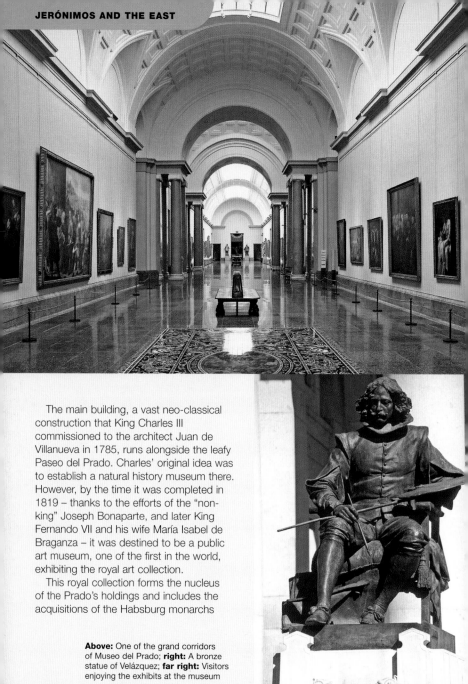

The main building, a vast neo-classical construction that King Charles III commissioned to the architect Juan de Villanueva in 1785, runs alongside the leafy Paseo del Prado. Charles' original idea was to establish a natural history museum there. However, by the time it was completed in 1819 – thanks to the efforts of the "non-king" Joseph Bonaparte, and later King Fernando VII and his wife María Isabel de Braganza – it was destined to be a public art museum, one of the first in the world, exhibiting the royal art collection.

This royal collection forms the nucleus of the Prado's holdings and includes the acquisitions of the Habsburg monarchs

Above: One of the grand corridors of Museo del Prado; **right:** A bronze statue of Velázquez; **far right:** Visitors enjoying the exhibits at the museum

VELAZQUEZ

from the 15th to the 17th centuries, as well as the later purchases of the Bourbons, on the throne from the 18th century onwards. In addition to this, later acquisitions of masterpieces have increased and enriched the Prado's holdings, be they works coming from other museums that have now closed or from numerous legacies and donations.

The major European schools of art are represented, with Spanish artists – most notably court painters Velázquez and Goya – featuring prominently. From the Spanish School also are works by El Greco, Ribera, Zurbarán, Murillo, the Madrazos, Rosales and Sorolla, among others. Various Italian schools are amply represented by Renaissance painters Fra Angelico, Mantegna, Antonello da Messina and Botticelli, with the next two centuries featuring works by Titian, Tintoretto, Veronese, Il Bassano and Raphael (16th century) as well as Luca Giordano, Corrado Giaquinto and Giambattista Tiepolo (17th century). Flemish painting is comparably well represented too, with masterpieces by Rogier van der Weyden, Hans Memling, Joachim Patinir, Quentin Metsys (or Massys), Bernard van Orley, Hieronymus Bosch, Pieter Brueghel, Rubens, Jordaens and Anton (Anthony) van Dyck. The fourth important group of works is that of the French artists, with an incomplete but highly interesting overview of 16th- and early 19th-century works as well as a more comprehensive selection of pieces from the 16th and 17th centuries. Outstanding amongst these are the works by Nicola Poussin and Claude Lorrain. The Germans are less well represented, but nevertheless there are important examples by Dürer and Anton Raphael Mengs. Some 200 works, principally from the 18th century, represent Dutch art, among them Rembrandt's masterpiece Artemisa.

Above left and left: There is much to see outside as well as inside this important museum

Parque del Retiro

This hugely popular park occupies almost 130ha (some 300 acres) and has more than 15,000 trees – it is effectively central Madrid's lungs. In addition, the Retiro also boasts many attractions and architectural embellishments.

The park was laid out during the 1620s and 1630s as the gardens of the Palacio del Buen Retiro, a palace built by the Conde-Duque de Olivares for Philip IV. It was intended to be the envy of Europe

Above: Visitors enjoying an afternoon stroll in Parque del Retiro

✚ **103 D4**

✉ **Parque del Retiro**
Bounded by Calle Alfonso XII, the Plaza de la Independencia and Calle Meléndez Pelayo

🕐 May–Sep 7am–midnight; Oct–Apr 7am–10pm

✋ Free

🚇 Retiro, Atocha, Príncipe de Vergara or Ibiza

– gardeners from all over the continent participated in the design and layout of the park, including a lake that is still there. From 1767, Charles III allowed the public limited access. After the fall of Isabel II in 1868, it was opened up entirely to the people of Madrid.

Towards the northern end is the boating lake, the *estanque*. Along one side, especially at weekends, there are performers of all types – tarot readers, cartoonists who will create your caricature on the spot, men in traditional Madrileño

Above: A stunning view of the Palacio de Cristal; **left:** The statue in the park, adjacent to the Casón del Buen Retiro, is the only reminder of Buen Retiro Palace dating from the 17th century

chulapo garb hawking *barquillos* (wafers), and usually a great throng of passers-by. Across the lake is the monument to King Alonso XII, a huge circular construction with steps leading down to the water on one side while a colonnade flanks the other. In the centre, atop a high plinth, is an equestrian bronze statue of the monarch, the work of Mariano Benlliure.

A little to the south of the lake, amid the trees, are two attractive buildings – both the work of architect Ricardo Velázquez Bosco, known for his "emphatically eclectic" style. The first is the Palacio de Velázquez, a pretty brick-and-tile pavilion with a glass and iron roof which was was built for an 1883 mining exhibition. On a grassy knoll nearby beside another small lake, out of which grow bald cypress trees, is the Palacio de Cristal, a gorgeous glass pavilion erected for the 1887 Philippines Exhibition. Both are now used as outposts for the

Reina Sofía Museum and make wonderful exhibition spaces.

Close by, continuing southwards, is a most singular monument: a statue depicting the *Fallen Angel*, sculpted by Ricardo Bellver in 1878.

A short distance due west of here, in the *chopera* (poplar grove) towards the southwest quadrant of the park, is the Retiro's most recent monument. This is El Bosque de los Ausentes, the Forest of the Departed – a man-made hillock bearing 192 cypress and olive trees, planted in memory of the 191 people killed in the 11 March bombings and the special agent who died during a police operation to arrest seven of the suspected perpetrators a month later.

The Retiro is a fabulous spot at all times of the year, both for energetic pursuits (such as jogging or rowing) and for spending a quiet moment on a bench with a book or just watching the world go by.

Plaza de Cibeles

Nobody visiting Madrid can fail to pass through – at least once during their stay – this four-way intersection, the nerve centre of the city. The statue of the goddess Cybele and the accompanying fountain in the centre, plus important buildings on each of the four corners, make the Plaza de Cibeles as emblematic to Madrid's inhabitants as the Eiffel Tower is for Parisians.

A little more than halfway from Sol to the Retiro, Plaza de Cibeles is the meeting point of the Calle de Alcalá, the northern end of the Paseo del Prado and the beginning of the Paseo de Recoletos. This area, full of gardens and fountains made for strolling in, was laid out in the late 18th century in the space occupied by the *prados* (fields) of San Jerónimo and Atocha, formerly called Prado Viejo (old Prado).

The iconic statue and fountain – designed by Ventura Rodríguez and completed in 1792 – depicts Cybele, the Roman goddess of fertility. Her origins go back further than the Roman empire though, to the Hittite and Phrygian cultures; she was also worshipped in Anatolia and ancient Greece. Cybele is represented here on a chariot drawn by lions which, according to mythology, represent Hippomenes and Atalanta who were

punished by the goddess Aphrodite and forced to pull this chariot until the end of time. The fountain was part of the Salón del Prado project to create a recreational space for all Madrileños.

Two other fountains, featuring Neptune and Apollo, were placed further down the Paseo del Prado. Cybele herself was originally placed in the Paseo de Recoletos, next to the Palacio de Buenavista but, towards the end of the 19th century, she was moved to her current location.

Today the magnificent buildings on each corner of the square enhance its importance as a key Madrid location. Going clockwise, they are: the Palacio de Buenavista (the Army headquarters), the Palacio de Linares (home to the Casa de América), the Palacio de Comunicaciones (formerly the city's central post office, now the new City Hall) and the Central Bank of Spain (Banco de España).

Nowadays, Real Madrid fans congregate in the Plaza de Cibeles to celebrate whenever the team wins a trophy. This has become a problem, as the Cybele statue has been damaged on numerous occasions and the authorities have had to set up fences to stop fans (and players) from bathing in the fountain.

Above left: The awe-inspiring Fuente Cibeles; **above right:** The goddess of nature riding a chariot, designed by Jose Hermosilla and Ventura Rodriguez

✚ **103 B3**

✉ **Plaza de Cibeles**
Plaza de Cibeles

🚇 Banco de España

Plaza de la Lealtad

This "square" in semi-circular form has two buildings worthy of note. The plaza itself backs up to a certain sober memorial that goes unnoticed by many visitors, as they reserve their awe for the Cybele and Neptune fountains and the Thyssen Museum which flank it.

About halfway down the Paseo del Prado, between the Plaza de Cibeles and the Neptune fountain, practically opposite the Thyssen Museum, stands one of Madrid's lesser-known monuments. On the left-hand side as you walk down is an obelisk, 46m (150 feet) high. It stands on the same spot where, on 3 May, 1808, the French general Murat ordered the execution of many Madrileños who had participated the day before in the popular uprising against the occupying forces. After various attempts to erect a monument to the victims, the obelisk was finally inaugurated on 2 May, 1840. In November 1985, the permanent flame that now burns there was lit and the monument was renamed by the current king, Juan Carlos I. It now commemorates all those who have fallen for Spain both in domestic and international conflicts.

At the base of the monument, which was designed by the architect Isidro González Velázquez, is an urn that contains the ashes of the fallen. A little higher up, a medallion represents in bas-relief the effigies of Luis Daoíz and Pedro Velarde, the army captains who led the rebellion.

The Plaza de la Lealtad, in a semi-circular form behind the memorial, contains two buildings of a different sort of importance. One of them is the Bolsa de Madrid (the city's stock exchange) which is housed in a neo-classical palace designed by Enrique

Repullés and inaugurated by Queen María Cristina in 1893. The other is the Ritz Hotel, which opened in 1910 and represents a project in which King Alfonso XII took a great deal of personal interest. It was his desire for Madrid to be able to offer its visitors something quite extraordinary – a hotel that could satisfy the refined taste of a new breed of traveller, who at that time was only just beginning to be known as a "tourist".

Below: The Mayo Obelisk at Plaza de la Lealtad

Puerta de Alcalá

Sitting on a traffic roundabout in the middle of the Plaza de la Independencia is the Puerta de Alcalá, the enormous city gate built in Colmenar stone with three Roman arches in the centre and two rectangular ones on either side. This grand monument is one of Madrid's principal emblems and, illuminated at night, it is truly spectacular.

It was not always so grand. In 1559, in order to commemorate the entry of Doña Margaret of Austria (wife of Philip III) into Madrid, a gate was built and named the Alcalá Gate – after the road, now called Calle de Alcalá, that led to the city of that name. But when Charles III entered Madrid in 1759, he was less than impressed by the existing gate, ordering its demolition in 1764 and calling on architects to present their ideas for a replacement. The king

studied the proposals, turning down no fewer than five by Ventura Rodríguez, eventually choosing those of Francesco Sabatini. Sabatini had proposed two different ideas. As Charles was taken with them *both* and could not decide which one he preferred, he commissioned Sabatini to

✚ **103 C3**

✉ **Puerta de Alcalá**
Plaza de la Independencia s/n

🚇 Retiro

Above: The Puerta de Alcalá with its Roman arches

Above: A night view of Puerta de Alcalá

build a gate that would incorporate both designs – one on each side.

This fact is often lost on visitors and Madrileños alike, but is easily noticeable if you contemplate each side carefully. The eastern side has ten columns while the western side has only two, employing pillars instead. Above the arches on the eastern side are three heads, each of a bearded man; the cornices have young boys bearing arms; and over the central arch, there is the royal coat of arms. On the western side, meanwhile, above the arches are three lions' heads; the cornices have representations of helmets, standards and shields; and over the central arch is depicted a flag and more helmets.

Construction began in 1774 and was completed in 1778, with Roberto Michel's sculptures and Francisco Gutiérrez's design for the coat of arms of the Bourbon dynasty. Since that time, the Puerta de Alcalá has stood witness to Spain's – and Madrid's – often turbulent history and bears the scars to prove it. Deep trenches were dug around the gate and a furious pitched battle was waged around the Puerto de Alcalá during the War of Independence in 1808; the marks remain to this day. So does the damage from cannon fire during the second French invasion of 1823. A political assassination took place by the gate in 1921 – that of Eduardo Dato, prime minister, who was gunned down by anarchists. However, no further damage was wreaked on the gate while Madrid was besieged in the Civil War. Franco's troops did not bombard it as many of his supporters lived in the nearby wealthy Salamanca district.

Real Fábrica de Tapices

King Philip IV founded the Royal Tapestry Factory in 1721. Philip called upon a family of weavers from Antwerp, headed by Jacobo Vandergoten the Elder, who established the first factory. In 1734, Jacobo Vandergoten the Younger opened a second factory in Madrid. The two were merged in 1744, with the king undertaking to meet expenses, thus setting in motion an industry linked to the Crown and financed by the public treasury.

In the 18th century Charles III appointed chamber painter Anton Raphael Mengs as artistic director. Mengs fostered the creativity of painters such as José del Castillo, Francisco Bayeu and Francisco de Goya. These artists gave the factory's tapestry designs a new and original aesthetic.

In the 20th century, as demand from the Crown declined, tapestry weaving became less important. Works by avant-garde artists such as Picasso and Dalí did, nevertheless, inspire some marvellous tapestries and woven carpets.

Nowadays run as a non-profit foundation, the factory continues to produce tapestries, carpets and coats of arms.

Real Fábrica de Tapices

➕ **103 D6**

✉ **Real Fábrica de Tapices**
Calle Fuenterrabía 2

☎ 91 434 0550

🌐 **www.realfabricadetapices.com**

🕐 Mon–Fri 10–2, guided visits only

🎫 Free

🚇 Atocha Renfe or Menéndez Pelayo

Real Jardín Botánico

➕ **103 B5**

✉ **Real Jardín Botánico**
Plaza de Murillo 2

☎ 91 420 3017

🌐 **www.rjb.csic.es**

🕐 Nov–Feb daily 10–6; Mar and Oct daily 10–7; Apr and Sep daily 10–8; May–Aug daily 10–9. Closed 25 Dec and 1 Jan

🎫 Inexpensive

🚇 Atocha

Real Jardín Botánico

Madrid's botanical garden was installed in its current location, just south of the Prado Museum, in 1781 during the reign of Charles III.

In the 8.1ha (20 acres) of garden, divided into three areas, there are over 30,000 plants from all over the world. Spring and summer are the best seasons to visit but it is pleasant all year round. The exhibition greenhouse, inaugurated in 1993, is particularly interesting. Here you can observe over 1,000 species in the tropical, desert and subtropical areas.

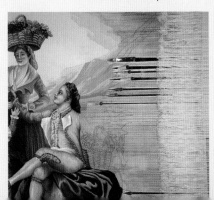

Below: A tapestry being made at the Real Fábrica de Tapices

San Jerónimo el Real

The original San Jerónimo el Real convent was founded in 1464, during the reign of Henry IV. It was located on the banks of the Manzanares, close to El Prado. However, owing to the excessive damp, it was relocated and rebuilt in Gothic Isabelline style for King Ferdinand and Queen Isabel only 40 years later, in 1503. It still stands today on a hillock just behind the Prado Museum.

From early on, the church was the site of choice for the swearing-in ceremonies of the Princes of Asturias, the heirs to the Spanish crown. The first of these was Philip II, sworn in on 18 April, 1528. He gave it even greater importance, and enlarged it after establishing his court in Madrid in 1561. During Philip IV's reign, from 1621 to 1665, underground passageways were dug connecting the church to the Casón del Buen Retiro. This was to allow the royals to go to the retreat they had had built in the eastern part of the monastery without drawing attention to themselves.

As it has been rebuilt several times few original external features remain. During the War of Independence, the French expelled the monks and requisitioned the monastery to quarter their troops, with major damage resulting to the building. The church itself was practically laid waste and

required extensive rebuilding work, which took place in several stages from 1848 to 1883. During the first phase, the towers were added by Narciso Pascual Colomer. The final stage of the restoration saw its conversion to a parish church.

More recent changes include the stairway that faces the street, built in 1906 to provide more impressive access to the church for Alfonso XIII's wedding and, in the early 21st century, the controversial demolition of the cloisters to make way for Rafael Moneo's "cube", which is part of the Prado extension.

Inside, there are paintings by Carducho and José Méndez, sculptures such as Juan de Mena's 18th-century *Cristo de la Buena Muerte*, as well as some neo-Gothic lamps and stained-glass windows.

Above: Detail of a statue at San Jerónimo el Real

✚ **103 B4**

✉ **San Jerónimo el Real**
Calle Moreto 4

☎ 91 420 3078

🕐 Mon–Sat 10–1, 5–8, Sun 9:30–2:30, 5:30–8:30

💵 Free

Ⓜ Banco de España or Retiro

Chueca and the North

Here we look at the central, older *barrios* (neighbourhoods) of Chueca and Malasaña, and the neighbourhoods collectively known as the Chamberí, lying to the north of the wide east–west main road that is called (at different points) Calle Carranza, Calle de Sagasta and Calle Génova. The first two districts, Chueca and Malasaña, have the irregular street layout characteristic of the city until the late 19th century and contain many historic sights, such as the mid 18th-century San Anton church. Chamberí, and Salamanca (its more glamorous neighbour across the Castellana) are much more recent, products of the post-1860s expansion and laid out in a gridiron pattern. This mixture of old and new is what makes for some fascinating sightseeing.

CHUECA AND THE NORTH WALK

1. Sala de Exposiciones del Canal de Isabel II
See page 144

From Ríos Rosas metro station (line 1), walk down Calle de Santa Engracia to the entrance of the offices of the Canal de Isabel II, Madrid's water company. You'll need an ID to get in and, with a "*visitante*" sticker on your lapel, you can head for the water tower, which is now a fabulous exhibition space.

2. Museo Sorolla See page 139

Continue down Calle de Santa Engracia to the Glorieta del Pintor Sorolla. Turn left and go down Paseo del General Martínez Campos. Don't miss the splendid semi-circular mansion on the corner of Calle Zurbano. Half a block on, at number 37, is another elegant mansion, where the painter Joaquín Sorolla lived and worked, which is now a charming museum dedicated to him.

3. Museo de Escultura al Aire Libre
See page 133

Now proceed to the Glorieta de Emilio Castelar at the intersection of Martínez Campos and the Castellana. Take the tree-lined boulevard and walk south towards the road bridge that crosses the Castellana. Under it, on the left-hand side, you will notice a collection of abstract sculptures – Madrid's Open-Air Sculpture Museum.

4. Plaza de Colón See page 142

Continuing down the Castellana – do peek at the elaborate façade of the ABC Serrano shopping mall on your left – you arrive at the Plaza de Colón (Columbus as the Spanish known him). A tall neo-gothic monument commemorates the explorer. Most of the square is given over to the Jardines del Descubrimiento, though. The twin tower blocks on the western edge are interesting – joined by a platform at the top, the structure atop them resembles a two-pin plug.

5. Plaza del Dos de Mayo See page 143

From Colón, walk west up the Calle de Génova, and then Sagasta, to the Glorieta de Bilbao – or if you are tired, take the metro (it's only two stops away). In Bilbao, have a coffee at the classic Café Comercial before heading down Calle de Manuela Malasaña. Turn left down either San Andrés or Ruiz and enter the Plaza del Dos de Mayo, heart of the grungy but slowly gentrifying Malasaña neighbourhood.

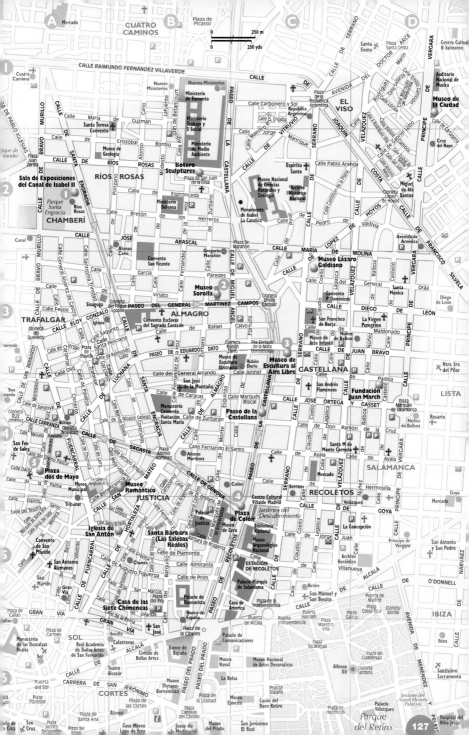

Below: Botero's the *Mano* is striking on Madrid's Paseo de la Castellana

Botero Sculptures

Anyone who was in Madrid during the late spring and summer of 1994 could not have failed to come across the show of sculptures by the Colombian painter and sculptor Fernando Botero, which were exhibited along the Paseo de Recoletos (between Cibeles and Colón). The hugely popular exhibition, which caused traffic to slow down as crowds flocked to see it, has since moved on; but three of the pieces are now on permanent display.

Born in Medellín in 1932, Botero's main focus is on "situational portraits". In the 1994 exhibition, there were some 21 huge bronze sculptures, many depicting splendidly rotund women in various poses, unabashedly showing their ample, rounded bosoms and buttocks, thus justifying the nickname given to the exhibition – Gordas, or Fat Ladies. Of the pieces now on permanent display, two are in Madrid city (the third, the *Reclining Woman*, is at Barajas Airport).

Botero decided to donate one of his sculptures to Madrid – the *Woman with Mirror* who lies across from the Plaza de Colón. Some way further up the Castellana, is the *Mano*, a huge left hand with delightfully plump fingers. This one was bought by Telefónica, the telephone company, and is on loan to the city.

Casa de las Siete Chimeneas

The name of this building means the "House of the Seven Chimneys". Seven chimneys stand on the roof of this late 16th-century palace, apparently placed there by order of King Philip II to represent the seven cardinal sins. As one of the few remaining examples in Madrid of civil architecture of that period, the building was declared a historic-artistic monument in 1948.

The palace was built between 1574 and 1577, by the architect Antonio Sillero. It has since then been renovated and enlarged many times. Interestingly, in 1882, the façade was altered to look more like it did when originally built.

The Casa de las Siete Chimeneas now houses the Spanish ministry of culture. It is not like a museum, however, open to the public – entry is reserved only for people who have business at the ministry.

The building is said to be haunted by the ghost of a woman who – so it was rumoured – was the secret lover of King Philip II. After her death, many people swore they saw a woman wandering around on the rooftop. The rumour is maybe not so far-fetched – during building work in the 1880s, a female skeleton was unearthed, accompanied by some coins dating from Philip II's period.

Botero Sculptures

✚ **127 B2**

✉ **Botero Sculptures**
Plaza de Colón and Paseo de la Castellana (opposite Plaza de San Juan de la Cruz), respectively

🕐 Daily 24 hours

💷 Free

🚇 Colón and Nuevos Ministerios, respectively

Casa de las Siete Chimeneas

✚ **127 B5**

✉ **Casa de las Siete Chimeneas**
Plaza del Rey 1, Calle de las Infantas 31

🚇 Banco de España

Fundación Juan March

Established in 1955 by Mallorcan financier Juan March Ordinas, the Fundación Juan March is one of the most important private art foundations not only in Spain, but in all of Europe. Its headquarters are in a modern building on the Calle Castelló, which is in the heart of the elegant Salamanca district.

Still family-run, the Juan March not only hosts major art exhibitions but also organises concerts, lecture series and seminars on many themes, among them poetry, philosophy and the social sciences.

The foundation also houses three specialist libraries that are frequented by academics and researchers. The Spanish Library of Contemporary Music and Theatre boasts a documentary collection of scenic art from the 19th century to the present day, in addition to its archive of contemporary Spanish music. The Julio Cortázar Library contains over 4,300 books and magazines – both by and about the Argentinean writer, who died in 1984. The Library of Illusionism has a collection of more than 1,700 works donated by José Puchol de Montís in 1988.

Besides these, the foundation is also home to the Centre for Advanced Study in the Social Sciences. Outside of Madrid, the Juan March Foundation also runs the Museu d'Art Espanyol Contemporani in Palma de Mallorca and the Museo de Arte Abstracto Español in Cuenca.

As there are usually three major art exhibitions every year, between September and late June, visitors have a good chance of coinciding their trip with one. They are usually monographic in nature, either featuring the work of one artist or that of a specific school or a particular period. In recent times, exhibitions have covered the work of Klimt, Roy Lichtenstein, Otto Dix, Turner and Kandinsky and themed collective shows on "The Spirit of Modernism", "Abstract Expressionism" and "Contemporary Spanish Art".

Concerts are free and are held at noon on Mondays, on Wednesday evenings and on Saturdays at midday – the Wednesday nights are the most popular. They usually feature soloists or chamber ensembles.

Above: Fundación Juan March

✚ **127 D4**

✉ **Fundación Juan March**
Calle Castelló 77

☎ 91 435 4240

🔲 www.march.es

🕐 Mon–Sat 11–8, Sun 10–2

✋ Free

🚇 Nuñez de Balboa

Iglesia de San Antón

Located on the corner of Calle Hortaleza and Calle de la Farmacia is the late 18th-century Escuelas Pías (pious schools), established in 1794 by the Escolapian fathers. The Iglesia de San Antón, though rather gloomy, is the most interesting part of the building.

This clerical religious order of the Escolapians had been founded in Rome, in 1600, by a Spanish-born priest, San José de Calasanz (1557–1648). They were bound to provide free education for all poor children. These schools were set up on land on which a lepers' hospital had once stood, run by the order of San Antonio Abad and dissolved by Pope Pius VI in 1791. Thus explains the name of the church.

The church was built by the great baroque architect Pedro de Ribera, being completed only a couple of years before his death in 1742. Sadly, little remains of de Ribera's work, as the outside of the church was rebuilt in neo-classical style by Francisco de Rivas

during Charles IV's reign. Only the interior gives away its baroque origin, with its rectangular ground plan and its semi-circular side chapels and short transepts.

Until 1990, the church's most precious possession was an 1819 Goya painting, *The Last Communion of San José Calasanz*, but this work now hangs in the Calasanz School on Calle Gaztambide, in the Chamberí district. The Escuelas Pías themselves had fallen into decay and were damaged by fire in 1995. However, they are now being revamped to house the College of Architects from 2009.

Without de Ribera's façade and the Goya, what remains to the church by way of an "attraction" is a bizarre carnival-like event

that takes place every year on 17 January. As this is the feast day of San Antón (or Anthony the Great), the patron saint of animals, the priest blesses dogs, cats, hamsters and sometimes more exotic pets brought in by locals. Farmers in the area even bring their donkeys in from the countryside.

Above: A priest blessing visitors at Iglesia de San Anton

✚ **127 B5**

✉ **Iglesia de San Antón**
Calle Hortaleza 63

☎ 91 521 7473

✋ Free

🚇 Tribunal or Chueca

Museo de la Ciudad

The purpose of this Museum of the City is to present an overview of Madrid's past, present and future – the last in terms of infrastructure projects that the authorities have in store for the city, as well as many others that have been carried out recently. It is a place for those with a particular interest in the history of urban development.

This museum was opened in 1992, Madrid's year as the European City of Culture. It is housed in a purpose-built structure next to the Auditorio Nacional de Música and little more than a stone's throw from Real Madrid's Bernabéu Stadium (Estadio Bernabéu).

The museum is arranged over four floors. The ground floor is basically a reception area, although itinerant and temporary shows of art and

Below: Madrid's "Gateway to the Sun", the Puerta del Sol

photography are sometimes put up here. The permanent exhibits start on the second floor. There visitors can look at the history of various infrastructural facilities that have helped Madrid become the great capital that it is now. Illustrative models show the growth of the water, gas, electricity, transport and telecommunications networks in fascinating detail.

The third floor takes us back to the origins of Madrid. The exhibits there explore the area from prehistoric times onwards. Particular attention is given to the Roman settlements that grew up close to Madrid, the original Muslim garrison town, the changes that came after the Christian reconquest, Madrid de los Austrias (Madrid under

the Habsburgs) and the expansion that came under the Bourbons.

On the fourth floor, we return to the 19th and 20th centuries. Highlighted here are some of the major events that affected civic development and properties. Among these are the uprising of 2 May, 1808, as well as important urban developments such as the Plaza de Oriente, the Puerta del Sol, the Ciudad Lineal, the Gran Vía and general suburban growth in the later 20th century.

Much use has been made throughout the museum of reproductions and architectural models of buildings and urban spaces, making the exhibits quite accessible even for children.

✠ **127 D1**

✉ **Museo de la Ciudad**
  Calle Príncipe de Vergara 140

☎ 91 588 6599

🌐 **www.munimadrid.es**
  (city council website)

🕐 Tue–Fri 9:30–8, Sat–Sun 10–2; closed Mon, public hols, 25 and 31 Dec, 6 Jan

✋ Free

Ⓜ Cruz del Rayo (line 9)

Museo de Escultura al Aire Libre

A museum for which no admission price is charged and which stays open twenty-four hours a day every day is not something you find just anywhere, but Madrid has one – the Open-Air Sculpture Museum.

Madrid's city traffic increased and its management became a problem during the 1960s. The authorities began to contemplate the building of an overpass that would take the traffic over the Castellana to join Calle Eduardo Dato on the western side (in the Chamberí district) and Calle Juan Bravo on the eastern side (in Salamanca). The engineers who were in charge of the project – José Antonio Fernández Ordoñez and Julio Martínez Calzón – did not stop just at designing an elegant bridge, however. They also decided that the area underneath would make a good space for art exhibits. Their idea helped make what could have been just another sterile, unexciting urban space into something a lot more interesting.

Fernández Ordoñez, along with the sculptor Eusebio Sempere got the ball rolling in 1970. This was shortly after the bridge itself had been inaugurated. The city council approved the plan in 1971, once the problem of costs had been resolved owing to Sempere's ability to convince a group of 15 fellow sculptors to donate pieces or create some especially for the space.

The collection shows the different tendencies at work within the Abstract movement in contemporary art, and many were designed specifically to fit into the space. One of the most spectacular is Eduardo Chillida's *Sirena Varada* – which means "beached, or stranded, mermaid" – a sculpture that dangles suspended from the bridge, despite weighing almost 6 tonnes. Just getting this sculpture into position was an engineering feat in itself. There are also pieces by artists as well known internationally as Joan Miró, Pablo Serrano, Martín Chirino, Marcel Martí and José María Subirachs. Lit up at night, this collection of sculptures is even more effective than in daylight.

Below: A large sculpture by the walls of Museo de Escultura al Aire Libre

✚ **127 C3**

✉ **Museo de Escultura al Aire Libre**
Paseo de la Castellana, 41

☎ 91 701 1863

🌐 **www.munimadrid.es/ museoairelibre**

🕐 Daily 24 hours

✋ Free

Ⓜ Rubén Darío

Museo Lázaro Galdiano

One of Madrid's lesser-known museums, the Museo Lázaro Galdiano contains a most extraordinary collection of some 15,000 paintings and other objets d'art that span almost 2,500 years of history. This collection was amassed during the long and prosperous life of the financier and bibliophile José Lázaro Galdiano (1862–1947), who lived in the impressive mansion that is now a museum.

✚ **127 C3**

✉ **Museo Lázaro Galdiano**
Calle Serrano 122

☎ 91 561 6084

🖳 **www.flg.es**

🕐 Mon and Wed–Sun 10–4:30

🖐 Moderate, free Sun

Ⓜ Gregorio Marañón or Rubén Darío

Left: *Saint John the Baptist in the Desert*, a painting by Hieronymus Bosch in Museo Lázaro Galdiano; **above:** *Witches Sabbath* by Francisco de Goya

Above: *Road from East Bergholt to Flatford* by John Constable; **right:** El Greco's *Saint Francis of Assisi*

The mansion itself is as much an asset to the museum as the collections. Commissioned by Galdiano in 1903, the project was initiated by the architect José Urioste. It was later remodelled and completed by Joaquin Kramer and Francisco Borrás in a neo-Renaissance style, with classical touches taken from Ventura Rodríguez. The pictorial decoration of the ceilings was commissioned to Eugenio Lucas Villamil, whose murals are full of mythological, literary and artistic allusions and portray Galdiano's intellectual make-up. The mansion was inaugurated in 1909 and was converted into a museum after Galdiano's death, opening its doors to the public on 27 January 1951. The museum then closed for a year in 2001, and reopened again in early 2004 after some tasteful renovation work had been carried out.

The 37 rooms spread over 3 floors are packed full of the most astonishing variety of pieces. Among the artworks on show here are paintings by English artists such as Gainsborough, Reynolds, Constable and Turner; lesser-known works by Goya, some from his "black period"; other Spanish masters such as El Greco, Velázquez, Zurbarán, Ribera and Murillo; and Italian painters such as Tiepolo and Guardi. There is also a canvas of *St John the Baptist* by Hieronymus Bosch.

Aside from the paintings there are any number of artefacts, including 15th-century hand-woven vestments, swords and daggers, royal seals, 16th-century crystal from Limoges, Byzantine jewellery, Italian bronzes from ancient times right up to the Renaissance, and medieval armour. A plus for non-Spanish speakers is that the labels on exhibits are in English as well.

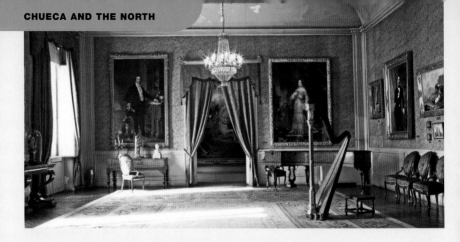

Museo Romántico

Tucked away in the narrow Calle San Mateo (between Calle de Fuencarral and Calle de Mejía Lequerica) is a characteristically small 18th-century palace that was built by Manuel Martínez for the Marqués de Matallana in 1779. It houses a fine museum today, remembering the Romantic era.

Though originally intended, and indeed used, as a private residence, the palace was let to the Marqués of Vega-Inclán in 1923 to be used as the head office of the tourist commission. However, in

Above: The interior of the Salon de Baile in Museo Romántico

✚ 127 B4

✉ **Museo Romántico**
Calle San Mateo 13

☎ 91 448 1045

🔳 **http://museoromantico.
mcu.es**

✋ Inexpensive

🚇 Tribunal or Alonso Martínez

1924 it was turned into a museum and was acquired by the state in 1927.

The museum – both in terms of its setting and the exhibits on show – evokes the essence of middle-class life in Madrid during the 19th-century Romantic period. On display is a charming array of household objects, including lamps, fans, porcelain furniture, ornaments, sculptures, busts, early pianos, books and documents – all laid out in different rooms. Some of the rooms include portraits of members of the royal family.

In addition, the walls are adorned with a good selection of paintings by some of the most important and renowned artists of

the time. One of them is Leonardo Alenza, two of whose finest paintings from 1839 are on show. Both of them satirise and ridicule the excesses of the Romantic period with their scornful portrayal of suicide. Federico de Madrazo, the finest portrait artist of the period, is also represented – by his *Portrait of María Bosch de la Presilla*. There is a Goya original too – a portrayal of St Gregory; and also a masterpiece by Valeriano Domínguez Bécquer, which portrays a Carlist conspirator.

Unfortunately, many of the exhibits were in need of restoration and the museum closed for extensive structural repairs in 2002. It is expected to reopen in 2009.

Museo Sorolla

Situated in the smarter end of the already pleasant Chamberí neighbourhood is this charming museum that was the home and atelier of the Valencia-born artist Joaquín Sorolla y Bastida (1863–1923). It was opened to the public as a museum in 1932.

The mansion, which Sorolla had built for himself in 1910–11 and where he lived until his death, was donated to the Spanish state by his widow, Clotilde García del Castillo. Conscious of the difficulties of working from home, Sorolla had separated the working areas from the living area. The working area comprised three studios with direct access from the garden and the living spaces had a large drawing room, a dining room and a smaller room on the main floor as well as four bedrooms on the second floor. A beautiful, tranquil house, it has large windows that let in plenty of natural light, an essential element in his painting.

On entering, it is worth lingering in the gardens, which are peaceful, quiet and provide welcome shade. They are mainly Andalusian-Moorish in style, with clear inspiration from the Gardens of Troy of the Reales Alcázares de Sevilla and the Generalife gardens in the Alhambra, though there are Italian elements also (such as the pergola). The lovingly laid-out gardens and the design of the house reflect Sorolla's desire to live close to the city – Chamberí at that time was considered suburban, but at the same time was well away from the hustle and bustle of central Madrid.

Though he trained in both Paris and Rome, Sorolla worked chiefly in Madrid.

Left: The exterior of Museo Sorolla

✚ **127 B3**

✉ **Museo Sorolla**
Paseo del General Martínez Campos 37

☎ 91 310 1584

🔲 **http://museosorolla.mcu.es**

🕐 Tue–Sat 9:30–8 (also mid-Jun to Sep 8–11:30pm), Sun 10–3

✋ Inexpensive, free Sun and for under-18s

🚇 Gregorio Marañón or Iglesia

His work thus reflects the historical realities and contradictions of a century that was drawing to a close. He has often been thought of as a neo-Impressionist, but it would be more accurate to describe him as an exponent of luminism, a style that made use of and positively celebrated light.

Sorolla became interested in painting the outdoors from a very early age – something he had in common with his French contemporaries – and would habitually stroll around orchards, gardens and along beaches. Such places were an important source of inspiration for his work. Though his subjects were often aristocrats, Sorolla was more interested in common people, whom he depicted in their daily attire, in family scenes, in gardens and at the beach.

He was also an expert in the feminine form, as can be seen by his portraits of women. In most of his work, bright Mediterranean sunlight is as much a protagonist as the people portrayed.

The museum contains in the region of 300 canvases, mainly on the second floor, and thousands of drawings scattered around the ground floor. In addition, there are exhibitions of other collections, pieces of sculpture, ceramics, jewellery, old photographs and an important archive of the artist's private correspondence.

Above: A statue of Joaquin de Sorolla; **right:** A small statue of a seated figure, set amidst greenery in the dappled shade in the gardens of Museo Sorolla

Paseo de la Castellana and Plaza de Colón

The Castellana, Madrid's grandest and longest avenue, runs several miles from the Plaza de Colón to Plaza de Castilla. It has enough attractions strung along its length to keep the most curious of visitors satisfied.

The avenue was created in the 1860s, as an extension of the already existing Paseos del Prado and Recoletos. It was envisaged as the main avenue of a new, chic residential district, the Ensanche (Extension), being laid out by Carlos María de Castro. And so it was soon lined with smart townhouses and villas.

The Castellana begins at the Plaza de Colón (formerly the Plaza de Santiago, renamed to celebrate the 400th anniversary of the exploits of Christopher Columbus, or Cristobal Colón as they call him in Spanish). Most of Colón is actually taken up by the Jardines del Descubrimiento (see page 106).

Until the 1930s, the Castellana only extended as far as Calle Joaquín Costa. However, one of the projects of the Second Republic from 1932 onwards was to relocate government offices by building the large, Kafka-esque Nuevos Ministerios on the site of the former racetrack. Consequently, the Castellana has extended to snake northwards through a forest of office blocks as far as the Plaza de Castilla and beyond.

There are many highlights along this great avenue. Just before reaching the Museo de Escultura al Aire Libre (see page 133) is the ABC Serrano shopping centre, located in the former offices of the ABC newspaper. It boasts rather a splendid façade. Opposite the Nuevos Ministerios complex is the Museo Nacional de Ciencias Naturales. Beyond the junction with Joaquín Costa, a huge branch of the Corte Inglés partially hides the AZCA business complex,

Left: Traffic on the tree-lined Paseo de la Castellana which runs past the modern, towering office blocks in the complex called Azca; **above:** An ultra-modern tower block set in Plaza de Colon

which is dominated by the impressive Torre Picasso skyscraper. A little further up, on the right-hand side, is Real Madrid's Bernabéu stadium. Finally, in the Plaza de Castilla itself are the leaning towers of the Puerta de Europa. The latest addition to this long avenue is the Cuatro Torres business complex beyond the Plaza de Castilla, its four thin skyscrapers dramatically changing the skyline.

Plaza del Dos de Mayo

This square in Malasaña takes its name from the date, 2 May, 1808, when the people of Madrid rebelled against the French occupying force of Napoleon's army. The neighbourhood itself is named after Manuela Malasaña, a seamstress executed by the French for carrying weapons (her scissors, in fact) to the Spanish troops.

On that day in 1808, fierce fighting erupted in the streets and carried on throughout the day, only to be followed by a period of brutal repression. The square was then the site of the Monteleon artillery barracks, where Captains Daoíz and Velarde orchestrated the resistance and died during it. There is a monument to the two men, but all that is left of the barracks is its gate, which is the arch in the centre of the square. The uprising was immortalised by Goya in his painting *The Charge of the Mamelukes*, which depicts the retaliatory repression that took place later that day in the Puerta del Sol.

In more recent years, the only battle to take place on the square is that between teenagers dedicated to the *botellón* (hard partying), the police and longsuffering residents – a skirmish that culminates on the public holiday marking the uprising. Gatherings were banned on the square for several years; but in 2007, things turned nasty with running battles between alcohol-fuelled youths and the police. However, in 2008, the event's bicentenary, the festivities passed off peacefully.

Below: Visitors seated under sun umbrellas at a street café in Plaza del Dos de Mayo

Paseo de la Castellana and Plaza de Colón

✚ **127 C4, 127 C5**

✉ **Paseo de la Castellana and Plaza de Colón**
Paseo de la Castellana (Plaza de Colón to Plaza de Castilla)

🚇 Colón, then bus 27 (runs the length of the avenue)

Plaza del Dos de Mayo

✚ **127 A4**

✉ **Plaza del Dos de Mayo**
Plaza del Dos de Mayo

🚇 Tribunal, Bilbao or Noviciado

Sala de Exposiciones del Canal de Isabel II

This exhibition space, which specialises in photography, always makes for an enjoyable visit – both for the splendid building as well as for the photographs. It is a converted water tower, built in the early years of the 20th century, and considered to be one of the finest examples of industrial architecture in Madrid.

The new building is in an elaborate and attractive neo-Mudéjar style. This is a unique architectural style that emerged in Madrid around 1870 and it is one that the city can claim as its very own. It was conceived by the architects Emilio Rodríguez Ayuso and Lorenzo Álvarez Capra who, tired of Roman, Gothic and Egyptian styles, decided to look back into Madrid's own history and found inspiration in the Mudéjar style, the architectural legacy of the Moors. They recreated the horseshoe arches, arabesque tiling and intricately interlaced brickwork that were so characteristic of Moorish building throughout Spain. The first neo-Mudéjar construction was a bullring that stood on the site where the Palacio de Deportes now stands in the Calle Goya. That bullring was demolished in 1934 and replaced by the Plaza de Toros de las Ventas (see page 153) which is also a fine example of the neo-Mudéjar style.

The Canal Isabel II water company stopped supplying the Chamberí district from the water tower in 1945. It then stood empty and abandoned until the mid-1980s, when it was given a new use – that of an exhibition space. So successful was the revamped water tower project that it won a Europa Nostra award. Since its inauguration in 1987, it has hosted many photographic exhibitions, featuring the work of Elliot Erwitt, Lee Freelander, Bernard Plossu, Garry Winogrand and Don McCullin as well as many collective shows. The pleasant gardens near the tower are technically not open to the public, but nobody seems to mind visitors to an exhibition taking a stroll there as well.

Above: Interior view of the converted water tower, now an exhibition space

✚ 127 A2

✉ **Sala de Exposiciones del Canal de Isabel II**
Calle de Santa Engracia 125

☎ 91 545 1000

🕐 Thu–Tue 11–8, Wed 11–3

✋ Free

Ⓜ Ríos Rosas

Santa Bárbara (Salesas Reales)

The convent of the Salesas Reales – whose grandiose official name is Monasterio de la Visitación de las Salesas Reales – and its church, the Iglesia de Santa Bárbara, were built on the initiative of Queen Bárbara of Braganza, wife of Ferdinand VI, in order to bring the Salesas nuns to Spain.

The architect in charge of the project was François Carlier, assisted by Francisco Moradillo. Carlier was absent during part of the construction period (1750–7), and so a number of changes in the original plan, such as the small towers on the façade and the dome of the church, can be attributed to Moradillo.

Both church and convent constitute an imposing example of the Spanish baroque architecture of the Bourbon period. The immense expense of it did not escape the notice of the locals, who summed it up humorously as *"Bárbara reina, bárbara gusto, bárbara obra, bárbara gasto"*, meaning "Queen Barbara, barbarous taste, barbarous project, barbarous spending".

Fernando and Bárbara are buried in the official and rather cold splendour of a tomb by Francisco Gutiérrez. Of the original buildings, only the church with its ornate frontage survives. In 1870, the nuns were expelled and the convent was converted into the Palacio de Justicia – which it is to this day, housing the Audiencia Nacional, or High Court. It burnt down in 1915, having already suffered a fire that destroyed the cupola in 1908. While it was being rebuilt in 1926, the architect Joaquín Rojí took the opportunity to give the building its present neo-baroque façade, looking onto the Plaza de la Villa de París. The church, which faces on to the Calle Bárbara de Braganza, shares the honour with San Jerónimos of celebrating most of the weddings in Madrid, many of them featuring high-profile brides and grooms at the altar.

Below: Trees and flowering shrubs in front of the granite façade of Las Salesas Reales

---

✝ **127 B5**

✉ **Santa Bárbara (Salesas Reales)**
Calle Bárbara de Braganza 3 and 5

☎ 91 319 4811

🕐 Convent Tue–Thu and Sat 10:30–12:30 and 4:00–5:30, Fri 10:30–12:30, Sun and public hols 11:00–1:30; church 8am and 7pm (during mass)

✋ Free

🚇 Colón

Further Afield

Madrid has grown enormously over the last century and a quarter. Small towns and villages that were once sleepy, rural retreats for city-dwelling Madrileños have now been engulfed by the city and are now just suburbs. To get an idea of this expansion, try to picture the 19th-century novelist Pérez Galdós going to Cuatro Caminos "to take the air". Cuatro Caminos is now a busy, traffic-choked neighbourhood, considered "central", just six stops on the metro from the Puerta del Sol. The periphery offers many attractions, among them the quiet leafy public parks, the brash, state-of-the-art theme parks, and sporting venues; royal palaces and thoroughly modern architecture – all easily accessible from the central core.

Aquópolis San Fernando

In a city like Madrid, where it gets fiercely hot in the summer and which is 320km (200 miles) from the nearest beach, water parks like Aquópolis provide a welcome and even necessary respite. It offers much-needed relief if you are in the city in summer with hot, fractious children, and it is fun for grown-ups too.

The Aquópolis at San Fernando de Henares is the first of two in the Madrid region (the other is in Villanueva de la Cañada).

✉ **Aquópolis San Fernando**
Carretera de Barcelona (Nacional II), km 15.5, San Fernando de Henares

☎ 91 673 1013

🖳 **www.aquopolis.es/san-fernando**

🕐 Jun daily noon–7, Jul–Aug noon–8, closed Sep to mid-Jun

✋ Expensive

🚌 Continental Auto 223, 227 and 229 from Avenida de América

It is relatively closer to the city and is easily accessible both by road and by bus.

The water park has many features – no fewer than 12 different attractions, in fact – and caters to all ages. For smaller children, there is a play area in which the little ones can run through jets of water that spurt upwards from the ground or play on the kiddie-sized slides. Nearby is a paddling pool for toddlers and those not yet able to swim with confidence. More assured swimmers who want the sensation of being in the sea can have fun in the wave pool. The lake, for just good old-fashioned swimming, is Europe's largest. Lifeguards are stationed everywhere, so there is no need to worry about your child's safety.

The more daring can hurtle in the dark down the Espiral, a coiled tube that throws you out at the bottom at great speed. Or test their nerves on the Kamikaze, a roller-coaster slide. There are also a variety of flumes; the Parabólico, a dish-like slide; and the long, undulating "soft slopes".

As you would expect in a park of this type, there are a range of refreshment facilities too, including a pizzeria, a hamburger joint, vending machines and ice-cream stalls as well as a small supermarket – if you forget your bathing suit, they sell those too.

Above: Children frolicking in the water at Aquópolis San Fernando

Capricho de la Alameda de Osuna

One of Madrid's least-known attractions, owing to its somewhat out-of-the-way location, the Capricho de la Alameda de Osuna is a real gem that should not be missed, even though a longish metro ride is needed to get there. The park and gardens are the whimsical creation – capricho is Spanish for "whim" – of Doña María Josefa Pimentel, 9th Duchess of Osuna (1752–1834).

An important grande dame of her epoch, the duchess directed the transformation of her country estate, which she had bought in 1783, into an elegant and romantic leisure garden. She and her husband, a cultivated couple, were enthusiastic promoters of the ideas of the Enlightenment and important patrons of artists, writers and musicians of the day. To be on the Osunas' guest list granted kudos and credibility to members of the aristocracy and intelligentsia in late 18th-century Madrid society, and the chance to socialise in a freer, more liberal ambience than that afforded by the stifling atmosphere of the court.

The duchess hired Jean-Baptiste Mulot, who had worked for Marie Antoinette, to execute a project initially proposed by the Spanish court architect Pablo Boutelou in 1784. The work took 52 years to finish and the duchess died without

seeing it completed, but it remains an outstanding and unique example of the landscape garden in Spain.

Small, formal gardens showing French and Italian influence alternate with English-style simulated "natural" landscapes. Fanciful constructions abound, among them a small palace in which numerous paintings by Goya once hung. A winding artificial river leads to a lake with islands in the middle, a jetty and a reed-covered boathouse. Look out for the small fort, the ballroom, the Greek and Egyptian temples (including one dedicated to Bacchus). Outstanding too is the Abejero, a pavilion designed to observe bees at work.

Now it is the property of the city of Madrid. The *Capricho* has been rescued from the state of decay and abandonment into which it had fallen and today it is open to visitors on Saturdays and Sundays.

Above: *Trachycarpus*, an ornamental palm, at the gardens

✉ **Capricho de la Alameda de Osuna**
Paseo de la Alameda de Osuna

☎ 91 588 0114

🕐 Apr–Sep Sat–Sun 9–9; Oct–Mar 9–6:30

✋ Free

Ⓜ El Capricho

Faunia

A fairly recent attraction, being set up in 2001, the Parque Biológico de Madrid, as it is correctly known, is neither a zoo nor a theme park but has many aspects of both. The aim of Faunia is, mainly, to educate adults and children about the world we live in, the other living beings that we share it with and the importance of conservation. This it achieves by a mixture of state-of-the-art technology and plenty of cuddly – and not so cuddly – animals. It makes for a great day out, if a slightly pricey one, for all the family.

The grounds occupy 140,000 sq m (166,500 sq yards) and contain many different climatic areas, with the animal and plant species corresponding to each ecosystem. These ecosystems range from tropical rainforests to and Mediterranean, evergreen and deciduous forests, from deserts to polar regions.

All the habitats are perfectly recreated at Faunia, both in terms of the vegetation and temperature as well as the animals inhabiting them. In all, there are over 4,500 animals of 720 different species and 72,500 trees of more than 1,000 types.

Add to this the aviary, the beehives, the butterfly garden, the "Territorio Wallaby", the Jurassic area and the exhibits on evolution, and you get an idea of the range of exciting things on offer.

Little children love the petting areas as well as the show put on by sea lions and seals in the lakeside theatre. Older children will appreciate the spectacle of eagles, falcons and vultures zooming over their heads in the same space.

Faunia certainly makes biodiversity and wildlife, in all its savage beauty, accessible to Madrid's urbanites. The facilities include dining areas, a nursery and an animal hospital. Though it's out in the eastern suburbs, Faunia is easy to get to by either metro or bus and is well worth a visit.

✉ **Faunia**
Avenida de las Comunidades 28

☎ 91 301 6210

Ⓦ **www.faunia.es**

Ⓒ Mid-Dec to mid-Jan daily 10–5:30; Feb Wed–Sun 10–6; Mar daily 10–6; Apr 10–7; May to mid-Sep daily 10–8; mid-Sep to end Sep Wed–Sun 10–8; Oct Wed–Sun 10–7; Nov to mid-Dec Thu–Sun 10-6; closed mid-Jan to mid-Feb

✋ Expensive

Ⓜ Valdebernardo (line 9)

Above: A brightly coloured toucan at Parque Biológico de Madrid or Faunia, just one of the many bird species here

Fuente del Berro

This charming park is another of Madrid's little-known treasures, being located as it is, on the eastern edge of the Barrio de Salamanca, at the far end of Calle Jorge Juan and flanked by the manic M-30 ring road – from which it is protected, thankfully, by sound barriers. It is not overly accessible, as the nearest metro stations are some distance away; however, the walk to the park takes you through a pleasant residential area consisting mainly of low-level housing, something of a rarity in Madrid.

The Fuente del Berro park dates back to the 17th century, when it was a cultivated plot that was especially fertile owing to the abundant water available there. In 1630, it was given in gift to King Phillip IV, who in turn donated it to the Montserrat monks of the Benedictine order 10 years later. In 1686, Queen María Luisa de Orléans issued an order to the effect that all water supplied to the royal palace must come from this estate.

Over the next two centuries, the land changed hands several more times. It was in the final years of the 19th century that a group of developers came up with a plan to build a sort of Champs Élysées, in line with the fashion for "attractions parks" then current throughout Europe. By 1897, a gateway, an office building, a greenhouse and a restaurant had been built; landscaping work – with pathways, rustic bridges and lake and waterfall – had begun. This project was never completed, though, as the plot was auctioned in 1902 and became a private garden once again – though more improvements were made, including the addition of an Andalusian-style garden and two streams.

In 1932, the city of Madrid acquired the park and declared it an "artistic garden" in 1948, opening it up to the public in 1951. Look out for the monuments to the Spanish poet Gustavo Adolfo Bécquer and the Russian writer Pushkin; also watch for the peacocks that wander freely.

Left: A peacock shows off its decorative plumes at Fuente del Berro

✉ **Fuente del Berro**
Calle Enrique D'Almonte

✋ Free

🕐 Summer 7am–midnight; winter 7am–10pm

🚇 O'Donnell (line 6) or Ventas (line 2)

Palacio Real de El Pardo

Lying to the north of Madrid, the Palacio de El Pardo is used as a residence for visiting foreign heads of state and as a monument open to the public. King Juan Carlos chose not to reside in the Pardo, which had been used by Francisco Franco as his official residence, on the dictator's death in 1975.

It is not to be confused with the nearby but totally inaccessible Palacio de la Zarzuela, the current royal residence, with which it

✉ **Palacio Real de El Pardo**
Calle Manuel Alonso s/n

☎ 91 376 1500

🔲 **www.
patrimonionacional.es/
en/elpardo/elpardo.htm**

🕐 Mon–Sat 10:30–4:45, Sun
10–1:30; gardens close 1
hour later

✋ Moderate

🚌 Intercity line 601 from
Moncloa bus station

shares 16,000ha (over 39,500 acres) of wooded parkland.

During the Middle Ages, this parkland, the Monte de El Pardo, was used as hunting grounds by the Castilian kings. Over the centuries, a small settlement grew up around it, including the Casita del Príncipe (the Prince's House), the convent of the Franciscan Conceptionists, and the Capuchin friary founded by King Philip III. (This last contains some notable works of art, including a sculpture of the *Recumbent Christ* by Gregorio Fernández and the *Virgin of the Angels* by Francisco de Rizi.

The general layout of the palace follows that of the medieval castle originally built on the site by King Henry IV of Castile. It was later rebuilt by the Emperor Charles V in 1553 and finished in 1558 during Philip II's reign, complete with a moat and a tower at each corner.

The interior decoration of the palace still conserves a ceiling painted by Gaspar Becerra during the reign of King Philip II, as well as paintings from King Philip

III's reign by artists such as Vicente Carducho (Vincenzo Carducci) and Cabrera. Also outstanding is the tapestry collection, all of which were woven at the royal factory, based on sketches by Bayeu, José del Castillo and Goya – the latter produced five of his best-known series for this palace. Other artworks displayed here include an equestrian portrait of Don Juan José de Austria by Julepe (or Jusepe) de Ribera and the *La Cuerna* by Diego Velázquez. There's also a collection of 18th- and 19th-century furniture.

Also worth visiting is the nearby *quinta* (country estate), formerly belonging to the Duque del Arco, which boasts wooded parklands and gardens interspersed with ornamental fountains. The interior of the mansion is decorated with 19th-century wallpaper, furniture, paintings and carpets from the reigns of Ferdinand VII and Isabel II.

Above: Interior of the El Pardo palace

Plaza de Toros de las Ventas

Going to a bullfight may not be on everybody's list of priorities when visiting Madrid. But whatever one's sensibilities regarding *la corrida*, as the bullfight is known, a visit to the spectacular bullring itself is of great interest for anyone with an interest in Madrid's architecture. La Plaza de Toros de las Ventas del Espíritu Santo, as the ring is officially called – though popularly abbreviated to Las Ventas – is a marvellous construction, built in the neo-Múdejar style that was popular in Madrid in the late-19th and early 20th centuries.

Above: Statue of a bullfighter on Plaza de Toros de las Ventas

⊠ **Plaza de Toros de las Ventas**
Calle de Alcalá 237

☎ 902 150025

www **www.las-ventas.com**

🕐 Box Office: Mar–Oct Fri 10–2, 5–8 (on fight days from 10am)

✋ Prices vary depending on seat location

Ⓜ Ventas

This style revives several aspects of Mudéjar architecture – the architectural legacy left behind by the Moors – among them horseshoe arches, arabesque tile work and intricate bricklaying techniques. Planned to replace the original bullring that stood in the nearby Calle Goya, the building Las Ventas was initiated in 1922 and completed in 1928, having cost four-and-a-half times the original budget. On 17 June, 1931, the inaugural *corrida* took place, a charity event that featured leading *toreros* of the day such as Diego Mazquirán "Fortuna", Manuel Mejías "Bienvenida" and Fausto Barajas.

With room for over 23,000 spectators, the massive ring is a fitting venue for a city that is considered to be the world's bullfighting capital.

Inside, in the centre is the arena or ring, which is where the action takes place. The seating area is divided into 10 *tendidos*, groups of 27 rows. In between are the patios, the area between the arena and the *barrera*, which is the fence behind which the spectators sit. Seat prices vary, depending on whether they are in the *sol* (sun) or *sombre* (shade) and how far up or down the *tendido* they are. This means that a seat at the top, in the sun, can cost a fraction

of a pricey ringside seat in the shade, so practically anyone can afford to "go to the bulls", as the Spanish call it.

Many people do not realise that there is also a small museum dedicated to bullfighting, called the Museo Taurino, which is behind the ring and beside the stables. Here you will see sculptures and portraits of famous matadors, as well as several *trajes de luces* (suits of lights), the bullfighters' outfits. One, pink and gold in colour, was worn by the legendary "Manolete" on the day that he died in the ring in 1947 – the bloodstains are still visible. Beside it is the blood-transfusion equipment used in the attempt to save his life.

Outside the ring are two statues of the toreros Antonio Bienvenida and José Cubero "El Yiyo", and also a monument depicting a bullfighter paying his respects to the bust of Alexander Fleming, whose great discovery – penicillin – has saved many a gored bullfighter's life.

Above: Spectators on Plaza de Toros de las Ventas; **right:** A matador with his bright pink cape at Plaza de Toros de las Ventas

Puerta de Europa (Torres KIO)

Approaching the Plaza de Castilla, whether coming from the north or the south, few are left unimpressed by the sight of these two towers that stand either side of the street, leaning towards each other at an angle of 14.3°. Not that everybody likes them – many public figures have derided them and a certain well-known newspaper columnist went so far to say that they were "so ugly".

Unlike the famous leaning tower in Pisa, Italy, these towers were of course *supposed* to lean – they constitute the world's first leaning high-rise buildings. They have been built over a metro interchange where three different lines pass through the Plaza Castilla station which meant that it was structurally impossible for the towers to stand closer to the street. Therefore architects Philip Johnson and John Burgee, responsible also for the AT&T Tower in New York, took the bold decision to make them lean towards each other so that they would "read" as a pair. The effect thus created is that of a portal, which – being at the very northern end of the business district – becomes a gateway to Europe, hence the name Puerta de Europa.

Construction began in the early 1980s and the bold, gravity-defying design was meant to symbolise a new economic dawn. Financing came from the Kuwait Investment Office (KIO, hence the name by which they are popularly known); but completion was delayed by over 10 years as a result of a financial scandal.

The towers each have 27 floors of offices. One of them is 1cm (0.39 inch) higher than the other. Each has a helipad on top, but one is green and the other red so that pilots do not get confused. Unfortunately, they are not open to the public – so visitors have to make do with gazing upwards.

✉ **Puerta de Europa (Torres KIO)**
Plaza de Castilla s/n

Ⓜ Plaza Castilla

Above: A view of Torres KIO at night

Real Madrid

In December 2000, Real Madrid was voted the best club of the 20th century by *FIFA Magazine* readers. Few can argue to the contrary, as the *Merengues'* honours list makes them one of the most successful football clubs on the planet.

The club was formed on 6 March, 1902, by Barcelona-born Juan Padrós Rubio, who assembled a team comprising players from a local student team and a splinter group from Foot Ball Sky to form the Madrid Foot Ball Club. They adopted the same kit as

✉ **Real Madrid**
Estadio Santiago Bernabéu, Avenida Concha Espina s/n

☎ 91 398 4370; ticket sales 902 324324

🖳 **www.realmadrid.com**

◔ Visits Mon–Sat 10–7, Sun 10:30–6:30

✋ Expensive

🚇 Santiago Bernabéu

Above: The Bernabeu Stadium (Estadio Santiago Bernabéu) is the home of Real Madrid

the London-based Corinthians FC – white shirts and shorts, purple socks – and played their first game three days later, using 37 substitutes!

The first official trophy came in 1905, after a 1–0 victory over Athletic Club Bilbao in the Spanish Cup final. It marked the start of a long, prolific journey. In 1920, King Alfonso XIII awarded the club the regal title of Real Madrid – although during the Second Spanish Republic, they had to revert to their original name.

When ex-player Santiago Bernabéu became chairman in 1943, the club underwent a colossal reformation. He initiated the construction of the Estadio Chamartín, which was inaugurated in December 1947 and renamed in his honour seven years later. He also built the legendary 1950s side with Francisco "Paco" Gento, Ferenc "Puskás" (Purczeld) and the club's greatest ever player, Alfredo di Stéfano. Between 1956 and 1960, Madrid claimed the first five European Cups. From

then onwards, rare was the season when they won no silverware. Today the club is has a loyal following worldwide.

Fans of the beautiful game cannot visit Madrid without visiting the impressive 80,000-seater stadium at the north end of the Paseo de la Castellana. The stadium is open to the public every day, except on match days when they close five hours before the game. Visits include a guided tour of the ground, dressing room, players' tunnel, trophy room and presidential box.

Book a tour either via ticket office number 10, next to Gate 7, or call 90 229 1709. Match tickets can be booked via the club's website (click on the "Next Game" tab) or directly from the box office, next to Gate 44, the day before the game.

Above: Real Madrid football souvenirs

Warner Bros Park

Inaugurated with much fanfare on 5 April, 2002, under the name of Warner Bros Park, the now renamed Parque Warner is located in the town of San Martín de la Vega, to the southeast of Madrid.

When first built, the park represented a commitment on the part of the regional government – which put up around 40 per cent of the initial investment – to create jobs and attract visitors to the Madrid region. Road and rail links to San Martín de la Vega were constructed especially to allow visitors ready access to this attraction. However, Parque Warner has not really lived up to its expectations and is reported to be losing money. For the visitor, though, none of that matters as a fun day out for all the family is guaranteed.

The park is divided into five themed areas, each offering a range of rides, souvenir shops and many establishments for eating and drinking – which is good, as you may not take your own comestibles in.

On entering, you first walk down Hollywood Boulevard, representing the mecca of film making. Here you can try Californian cuisine and splash out some of your cash on movie paraphernalia. In the Movie World Studios area, visitors can discover the secrets behind special effects and make-up, and then take in live shows of *Lethal Weapon* or *Police Academy*, complete with shoot-outs, chases and explosions. There are plenty of thrills and spills in the Superheroes World area, where you can pretend to be Superman and fly on "Superman/The Attraction of Steel" or go to Gotham City as Batman to fight a duel with the Joker on "The Vengeance of the Enigma".

Smaller children are usually delighted to meet their favourite cartoon characters, such as Donald Duck, Tweety and Bugs Bunny, at Cartoon Village. The Old West Territory, meanwhile, has some hairy rides in Wild West style, with huge wooden roller-coasters and perilous waterfalls.

Below: Warner Bros Park

✉ **Warner Bros Park**
San Martìn de la Vega

☎ 91 821 1234

🌐 **www.parquewarner.
com**

🕐 Check website for details;
closed weekdays
mid-Sep to Mar

✋ Expensive

Ⓜ O'Donnell (line 6) or
Ventas (line 2)

🚆 C3a from Atocha

Listings

Madrid might be a lot of things but what it most certainly is not is dull, a fact that is not lost on visitors. Back in its first century or two as the capital of Spain, it was a dark, dirty, dangerous and rather shabby city, one that lacked many of the trappings expected of a European capital. But even back then visitors commented on its extraordinary vitality and the theatricality apparent in its street life and on the grand occasions staged by the Court. Others remarked on the variety of high quality goods on offer in the city's shops, from Italian silk to fresh fish, brought in on ice from the coast, which positively shone out from the scruffy surroundings.

Much has changed since then, of course, but some things remain the same. Madrid continues to be anything but dull and that vitality is obvious to all. Restaurants are always bustling, late-night bars filled to capacity, people queue to get into clubs, and the streets of neighbourhoods like Chueca and Malasaña are usually thronging with people, even during the week.

Accommodation

Everyone, from backpackers to business executives, will find accommodation to suit their tastes and pockets in Madrid, at prices that will not make them baulk. The amount of accommodation on offer, and the quality, has gone up in recent years, partly in response to Madrid's ultimately unsuccessful bid for the 2012 Olympics and partly as a result of the city's growing importance as a business centre.

Prices for each hotel are a guide only, and are based on a standard double room for one night.

€ Under €75
€€ €75–€150
€€€ Over €150

CENTRO

Emperador Hotel €€€

This hotel has an excellent location right in the centre of Madrid. Its interior is lavish, with marble floors and plush velvet chairs. The outdoor rooftop swimming pool – with views across to the Palacio Real and Catedral de la Almudena – attracts well-to-do sun worshippers in the summer. There's also a restaurant, club lounge, sauna, gym, pool table, lobby bar, laundry, salon and parking. The Emperador has 232 majestic rooms, including junior suites and suites, all decked out in 19th-century Spanish style, with rich colours and chandeliers.

⊠ Calle Gran Vía 53
☎ 91 547 2800
🖳 www.emperadorhotel.com
🔲 Santo Domingo

Mayorazgo Hotel €€

A classical hotel with the old-fashioned feel of a 1940s film set, the Mayorazgo is popular with British tourists due to its numerous restaurants and central location, just a few metres from the main street of Gran Vía. The rooms are soundproofed, so guests can enjoy total peace and quiet whilst staying in a buzzing location.

⊠ Calle Flor Baja 3
☎ 91 547 2600
🖳 www.hotelmayorazgo.com
🔲 Plaza de España

Siete Islas Hotel €€

With a reception area resembling a tropical oasis, this hotel gains points for individuality. Its "Siete Islas" (Seven Islands) theme relates to the seven Canary Islands – each room is decorated in the style of a different Canarian village. Although the street it sits on isn't too attractive, the hotel's location is superb: on the edge of the gregarious Chueca district and less than one minute's walk from Gran Vía's shops, theatres and restaurants.

✉ Calle de Valverde 14
☎ 91 523 4688
ᵂ www.hotelsieteislas.com
Ⓜ Gran Vía

The Urban €€€

This is a seriously cool hotel. Its funkiest features include the designer rooftop pool and bar, unique Egyptian art and famous Glass Bar, frequented by the "It" crowd. In 2006, the Hotel Urban gained "grand luxe" categorisation from Madrid's General Board of Tourism. No other hotel in Madrid has achieved this in over 27 years. There are 96 rooms including 85 doubles, four singles, three junior suites and four suites and each is decorated in a clean cut, minimalist, but comfortable style.

✉ Carrera de San Jerónimo 34
☎ 91 787 7770
ᵂ www.hotelurban.com
Ⓜ Sevilla

Vincci Centrum €€

This is one of Madrid's trendiest designer hotels. It's in a superb location, just 5 minute's walk from Puerta del Sol in the city centre and Madrid's three most famous art museums – the Prado, the Thyssen-Bornemisza and the Reina Sofia. The hotel was fully refurbished in 2004. Each of its 85 rooms and two luxury suites encourages guests to live it up in style. The most impressive rooms offer balconies with breathtaking views of the city skyline.

✉ Calle Cedaceros 4
☎ 91 360 4720
ᵂ www.vinccihoteles.com
Ⓜ Sevilla

JERÓNIMOS AND THE EAST

Abba Madrid Hotel €€€

The Abba is on the fringe of Madrid's exclusive Salamanca district – access to the city centre by metro takes 15 minutes. Guests from the hotel enjoy free use of a nearby fitness centre and indoor swimming pool. There are 207 standard rooms, 22 executive rooms, 4 suites and 4 junior suites. The suites all have separate lounge areas, Jacuzzis and terraces with great views across the rooftops of Madrid.

✉ Avenida de América 32
☎ 91 212 5000
ᵂ www.abbamadridhotel.com
Ⓜ Cartagena

Arco Iris Hostal €

A recent refurbishment has made this a stunningly colourful hostal, with a summery theme running through its 10 rooms. There's a clean and modern feel overall, and the staff are helpful and friendly. Smoking is not permitted.

✉ Calle O'Donnell 27, 6° derecha
☎ 620 936 277
ᵂ www.hostalarcoiris.com
Ⓜ Príncipe de Vergara

Residencia Don Diego Hostal €€

This hostal is found inside a quaint and old-fashioned stone building in the prestigious Salamanca district, a short walk from the Parque del Retiro. It's great value for the area. The rooms are comfortable, and simply furnished with tasteful decor and wooden floors.

✉ Calle de Velázquez 45
☎ 91 435 0760
ᵂ www.hostaldondiego.com
Ⓜ Velázquez

Meliá Galgos €€€

Situated in the regal district known as Salamanca, the Galgos appeals to upmarket travellers and business people. Each of the 261 double rooms is decorated differently, but all have an inviting feel. There are also 43 single rooms and 5 luxurious junior suites too, and the hotel offers a pillow menu to all guests. The "Royal

Service Floor" offers added advantages in the form of a separate reception area, secretary on hire, private breakfast room and free buffet bar. There's ample opportunity to relax in the wellness centre, which includes gym, steam bath, sauna, massage room, UVA sunbeds, Jacuzzi and a solarium on the roof.

✉ Calle de Claudio Coello 139
☎ 91 562 6600
🖳 www.meliagalgos.com
🚇 Nuñez de Balboa

Wellington €€€

This hotel is fit for royalty, and it oozes quality. Fresco paintings adorn the reception walls and grand chandeliers hang from the ceiling. Perks for guests include a limousine service, a sauna, Jacuzzi, swimming pool and garden terrace.
There are 262 comfy and spacious rooms, and 27 grand suites with four-poster beds. The Parque del Retiro is less than a 5-minute walk away and the city centre can be reached within 10 minutes on foot from the Wellington.

✉ Calle de Velázquez 8
☎ 91 575 4400
🖳 www.hotel-wellington.com
🚇 Retiro

PALACIO AND THE WEST

Florida Norte Hotel €€€

This is a massive 400-room hotel with a sombre and serious feel. The hotel provides facilities for business travellers, but is also popular with tourists due to its location right across the street from a big shopping centre and the Princípe Pío train station. Rooms at the rear of the hotel look out over the Manzanares River, which is currently undergoing regeneration through a civic project.

✉ Paseo de la Florida 5
☎ 91 542 8300
🖳 www.hotelfloridanorte.com
🚇 Princípe Pío

Husa Moncloa Hotel €€

The Moncloa is situated to the west of the city centre and is part of a complex that also includes the Husa Princesa. The Moncloa is housed in one tower of a building that shares central facilities with the Princesa. Nightlife options come in the form of the attractive Global Bar with its outdoor terrace, the restaurant Malvasia (which serves Mediterranean cuisine) and a piano bar that specialises in cocktails.

✉ Calle Serrano Jover, 1
☎ 91 542 4582
🖳 www.hotelhusamoncloa.com
🚇 Argüelles

Intur Palacio San Martín €€

The stately feel of this hotel is due to the fact it was formerly a 19th-century palace. It has 86 classically decorated rooms, seven of which offer a hydro-massage shower. The hotel's elegant rooftop restaurant, the Antigua Embajada, serves up excellent national and international dishes. A perfect location for an evening stroll to the nearby royal opera house, the Teatro Real.

✉ Plaza de San Martín 5
☎ 91 701 5000
🖳 www.hotelinturpalacio.com
🚇 Ópera

Opera Hotel €€

This hotel's restaurant comes complete with opera-singing waiters, which makes for a unique dining experience! The hotel itself is right next to the royal opera house, Teatro Real, in the heart of Bourbon Madrid. Some of the city's most beautiful buildings are to be found in this area. The Palacio Real is just a 2-minute walk from here, as are the Sabatini gardens and the lush Plaza de Oriente. There are 79 rooms, some with hydro-massage bath and balcony.

✉ Calle Cuesta de Santo Domingo 2
☎ 91 541 2800
🖳 www.hotelopera.com
🚇 Ópera

Petit Palace Arenal €€

This boutique hotel offer 64 rooms, the snazziest of which come with a PC, exercise bike, valet press, hydro-massage shower and king- or queen-size bed. The rooms are sleek and modern with quirky touches such as jellyfish lamps!

✉ Calle Arenal 16
☎ 91 564 4355
ⓦ www.madridpparenalhotel.com
Ⓜ Sol or Ópera

Room Mate Mario Hotel €€

Room Mate is a chain of hotels built with design in mind. A black-and-white theme runs throughout this hotel, and the rooms are cleverly lit using designer lamps by Philippe Starck. There's free WiFi, flatscreen satellite TV and big, fat, fluffy towels in all rooms. The feel is über chic, making the hotel appeal to a super-cool crowd.

✉ Calle de Campomanes 4
☎ 91 548 8548
ⓦ www.room-matehotels.com
Ⓜ Ópera

CHUECA AND THE NORTH

Cuzco €€€

A tall and sleek-looking hotel with a serious ambience that caters very well for business visitors, the Cuzco is situated in the financial district and has good metro links to other parts of the city. The good news for football fans is that the hotel is only a 5-minute walk from the Real Madrid stadium.

✉ Paseo de la Castellana 133
☎ 91 556 0600
ⓦ www.hotelaccuzco.com
Ⓜ Cuzco

Meliá Castilla €€€

This huge hotel is reminiscent of a commercial centre, food hall, business centre and hotel all rolled into one. As it's only 20 minutes by taxi to the airport from the Meliá Castilla hotel, it's popular with business travellers and flight crews. There are several bars and restaurants here to cater for the mixed clientele, and 916 rooms in all, including 100 luxury rooms and 12 suites. Leisure travellers will love the outdoor pool.

✉ Calle Capitán Haya 43
☎ 91 567 5000
ⓦ www.meliacastilla.com
Ⓜ Cuzco

Orense €€–€€€

This hotel is in the AZCA business district of Madrid. The Real Madrid stadium is 5 minutes' walk away and there are plenty of local amenities. The hotel has 130 rooms, decorated in a modern cream and brown theme. The hotel has good access by metro to the city centre and the airport.

✉ Calle de Pedro Teixeira 5
☎ 91 597 1568
ⓦ www.rafaelhoteles.com
Ⓜ Santiago Bernabéu

Petit Palace Ducal €€

A cool and funky hotel in a cool and funky district of Madrid. The rooms are decked out in bright colours, while the restaurant is painted a striking black with red highlights. Top-range rooms boast gorgeous little terraces, which are worth paying extra for.

✉ Calle Hortaleza 3, corner with Calle Gran Vía 26
☎ 91 521 1043
ⓦ www.madridppducalhotel.com
Ⓜ Chueca or Gran Vía

Tryp Gran Vía €€

This is the place to stay for easy access to Madrid's theatres and main shops. The hotel also flanks the district of Chueca, known for its gay party atmosphere. The 175 rooms are spacious and pleasantly decorated in blues and yellows. Despite the bustle outside, the hotel is tranquil.

✉ Calle Gran Vía 25
☎ 91 522 1121
ⓦ www.solmelia.com
Ⓜ Gran Vía

Restaurants

Eating, and eating well, has always been a very important part of life for Madrileños and lunch is traditionally a serious affair, and worth taking your time over. But at the same time, in the past though a typical lunchtime menu was affordable and wholesome, it was hardly adventurous. It is still very much a serious thing these days too, what has changed is not the attitude to the business of eating but what is eaten and how. Whereas not long ago Catalan cooking or maybe a pizza was about as exotic as you'd get, nowadays people happily tuck into sushi, pad thai or chicken satay without batting an eyelid.

Prices for each restaurant are a guide only, and are based on a three-course meal from the menu for one person.

€ up to €15
€€ from €15–€30
€€€ over €30

CENTRO

El Alebrije €–€€
This is a bright and cosy Mexican restaurant with comfortable sofas by the window, where people sit and sip cocktails. There's a great cocktail menu of 64 drinks. Mariachis play live at the weekends.
✉ Calle del Espíritu Santo 36
☎ 91 522 6190
🔤 www.elalebrijedemadrid.com

🕓 Thu–Sat 1–4:30, 8–2, Tue–Sun 8pm–2am
🚇 Noviciado

Arrocería Gala €€
This restaurant is situated in what is essentially a conservatory. It's rather like being in a jungle, with plants everywhere. The whole "outdoor" feel is topped off with garden furniture and bright lighting. There are 10 types of paella, 5 risottos and more than 15 other rice dishes on offer.
✉ Calle Moratín 22
☎ 91 429 7621
🕓 Tue–Sun 1:30–4:30 and 9–11:30
🚇 Antón Martín

La Biotika €
This vegetarian, macrobiotic restaurant offers food based on an ancient yogic

diet, which contains no meat, fish, egg, lactose, garlic or mushrooms. The front of the building houses a health-food shop, and the clean and pleasant dining room is through to the rear. There's a different set menu each day, with dishes that are filling, full of flavour and very healthy.

- ✉ Calle Amor de Dios 3
- ☎ 91 429 0780
- 🌐 www.labiotika.es
- 🕐 Mon–Sat 10am–midnight, Sun 10–4:30
- Ⓜ Antón Martín

Botín €€€

Botín is listed in the *Guinness Book of Records* as the world's oldest restaurant – it dates back to 1725, which is evident from its narrow stairways and old-fashioned tiled walls. There are four storeys, each with a unique ambience, but the basement is always the busiest due to the roast suckling pig served there.

- ✉ Calle de Cuchilleros 17
- ☎ 91 366 4217
- 🌐 www.botin.es
- 🕐 Daily 1pm–4pm and 8pm–midnight
- Ⓜ La Latina

Casa Lucio €€€

Casa Lucio is a heaving restaurant with a long-standing reputation for excellent Madrileño food. Expect to find politicians, journalists and celebrities within its traditionally decorated walls. The dress code is smart and the meals are hearty.

- ✉ Calle Cava Baja 35
- ☎ 91 365 3252
- 🌐 www.casalucio.es
- 🕐 Sep–Jul Mon–Fri and Sun 1:15–4 and 9–11:30; Sep–Jul Sat and Aug Mon–Sun 9pm–11.30
- Ⓜ La Latina

Casa Mingo €

Established in 1888 in this cavernous space that used to be a railway warehouse, Casa Mingo is one of Madrid's most genuinely popular restaurants – a favourite with students celebrating post-exam and with families, because it is cheap and cheerful. The fare on offer is simple – roast chicken and salad (though you could have the chorizo in cider instead), washed down with cider and followed by Cabrales cheese.

- ✉ Paseo de la Florida 34
- ☎ 91 547 7918
- 🕐 Daily 11–noon
- Ⓜ Príncipe Pío

Don Pelayo €€€

Entry into this eatery is through the front bar area, then into a majestic rear dining room where – to compensate for the lack of windows – the walls are spruced up with fresco paintings showing beach and mountain scenery. The dignified atmosphere is reinforced by the waiters, who are immaculate in black jackets and bow ties. If you dine at Don Pelayo any day from Thursday to Saturday, an extra treat comes in the form of live music.

- ✉ Calle de Alcalá 33
- ☎ 91 531 0031
- 🕐 Mon–Sat 1–4:30 and 8–midnight
- Ⓜ Sevilla

Estragón €€

This vegetarian restaurant has a cosy candle-lit ambience, making it the perfect setting for a romantic dinner. The dishes are novel and include *crêpes a la mouselina* – a mammoth plate of three thick crêpes filled to bursting with various vegetables, quinoa and dried fruit, all coated in a creamy, garlicky sauce.

- ✉ Plaza de la Paja 10
- ☎ 91 365 8982
- 🕐 Mon–Thu 1–4:30 and 8–12:30am, Fri–Sun 1–4:30 and 8–1:30am
- Ⓜ La Latina

Lhardy €€€

This beautiful, old-fashioned restaurant has been open since 1839 and has played host to politicians, dignitaries and royalty. Its most well-known dish is the typically

Spanish cocido Madrileño, an elaborate type of stew made with chickpeas, meat and cabbage that is eaten in three parts. The downstairs space houses a patisserie and tapas bar.

✉ Carrera de San Jerónimo 8
☎ 91 521 3385
ⓦ www.lhardy.com
🕐 Mon–Sat 1–3:30 and 9–11:30, Sun 1–3:30
Ⓜ Sevilla

Medina Mayrit €€€

This is a place in the centre of Madrid where diners can first enjoy the hammam (Turkish baths) before eating in the restaurant and watching the belly-dancing show. The cuisine is a mixture of Spanish, Arabic, Andalusian and Jewish. Inside it's cosy and Moroccan in style.

✉ Calle Atocha 14
☎ 90 233 3334
ⓦ www.medinamayrit.com
🕐 Daily 1:30–4 (lunch), 5–8 (tea room) and 10pm–midnight (dinner)
Ⓜ Sol or Tirso de Molina

Negro de Anglona €€€

The dining area of this restaurant is literally inside a tunnel. The tunnel was built to lead into the former Palacio de Anglona – at one time kings used to creep along it on their way to visiting their various mistresses. There's a stately feel to this restaurant, due to the large doors with their coats of arms and the palatial salons. The colour scheme is mainly black and the food is Mediterranean fusion.

✉ Calle Segovia 13
☎ 91 366 3753
ⓦ www.negrodeanglona.com
🕐 Mon–Thu 9pm–1am, Fri–Sat 2–4, 9pm–2am, Sun 2–4
Ⓜ La Latina

Nippon €€–€€€

This is a Japanese restaurant with a Zen-like feel – low tables and shelves of traditional sandals. The tempura vegetables

are a popular choice with the boho crowd that dines here. Nippon's green tea is the perfect way to finish off a satisfying meal.

✉ Calle de los Madrazo 18
☎ 91 360 0354
🕐 Daily 1:30–4 and 8:30–midnight
Ⓜ Sevilla

Pink Sushiman €

The strangely named Pink Sushiman resembles a spaceship, with its chrome and Lucite walls and its sleek white booths. Small servings of maki, sashimi and salads cruise by on a kaiten (a conveyor belt). Dishes are priced depending on the colour of the plate. This is a novel and ultra-modern place to grab dinner.

✉ Calle Caballero de Gracia 8
☎ 91 360 5608
ⓦ www.pinksushiman.com
🕐 Daily 1:30–midnight
Ⓜ Gran Vía

Pinocchio €€

This is a cheap and cheerful place situated on the opposite side of the square from the Reina Sofia museum. The food is basic but tasty. The menu includes dishes such as lasagna, pasta, meat and salad. There's a pleasant terrace shaaded by trees, which is peaceful as the area is pedestrianised.

✉ Calle Sánchez Bustillo 5
☎ 91 468 7373
ⓦ www.pinocchio.es
🕐 Mon–Thu and Sun 12:30–12:30; Fri–Sat 12:30pm–1:30am
Ⓜ Atocha and Antón Martín

Viva la Vida €

There's alfresco dining at this tiny vegetarian health-food shop with its "eat in or take away" buffet. Diners pay by the weight of their plates – and it's easy to get carried away, such is the choice of hot and cold dishes! Top marks to the food for its healthiness alone, never mind the mouth-watering mixture of flavours.

✉ Calle de las Huertas 57

☎ 91 369 7254
🕐 Daily 11am–midnight (also Fri–Sun till later if busy enough)
🚇 Antón Martín

JERÓNIMOS AND THE EAST

Acquafredda €€
This is a stylish Italian restaurant owned by Ignazio Deias, who also presides over Per Bacco, Piazzetta and Ma Tutti. Inside the restaurant is a huge deli, stocked full of Italian products. There's also a pastry counter and an impressive wine cellar. The food is fresh and portions ample.
✉ Calle Maldonado 15
☎ 91 411 6314
🕐 Tue–Sat 10am–11:30pm, Sun 10–4:30
🚇 Núñez de Balboa

Alfredo's Barbacoa €
Alfred Gradus, an ex-pat from the Bronx, is famous for making the best burgers, BBQ ribs and other American specialities in Madrid, not to mention the delicious home-made desserts.
✉ Calle Lagasca 5
☎ 91 576 6271
🌐 www.alfredos-barbacoa.es
🕐 Daily 1–1
🚇 Retiro

Loft 39 €€€
The elegant and fashionable set goes to Loft 39. It's all about design here, both in terms of the decor as well as the style and presentation of the food. The speciality is internationally acclaimed wagyu beef.
✉ Calle de Velázquez 39
☎ 91 432 4386
🌐 www.restauranteloft39.com
🕐 Daily 1:30–4, 9–midnight; bar-lounge daily 1pm–2am
🚇 Velázquez

Nicolás €€
This is a posh restaurant in the exclusive district of Salamanca that serves traditional

Spanish fare. The menu is hand-written, and among the dishes are pheasant, quail and chickpeas, all cooked in a creative way.
✉ Calle de Villalar 4
☎ 91 431 7737
🕐 Sep–Jul Mon–Sat 1–4 and 9–midnight, Sun 1–4; closed Aug
🚇 Retiro

PALACIO AND THE WEST

Belalúa €€€
Belalúa is a very stylish eatery. Demure business types and well-heeled locals frequent the premises in order to enjoy the Asturian and Galician cuisine here. The food, the service and the tasteful contemporary decor are the epithet of unfussiness and elegance.
✉ Calle de San Nicolás 8
☎ 91 547 2222
🌐 www.belalua.com
🕐 Mon–Sat 1:30–4, 8:45–midnight, Sun 1:30–4
🚇 Ópera

Casa Ciriaco €€–€€€
Located in the old part of Madrid, this is a traditional restaurant with old-fashioned food. It used to be a meeting place for intelligence officers before the Civil War, but now the main reason to visit is to taste the suckling pig and enjoy the friendly service.
✉ Calle Mayor 84
☎ 91 548 0620
🕐 Thu–Tue 1–4, 8–midnight; closed Aug
🚇 Sol or Ópera

Casa Marta €€
This is another place to try traditional Spanish food such as scrambled eggs, ham, bacon and chorizo sausage.
✉ Calle de Santa Clara 10
☎ 91 548 2825
🌐 www.restaurantecasamarta.com
🕐 Sep–Jul Tue–Sat 9pm–midnight, Mon 1:30–4:30; closed Aug
🚇 Ópera

Taberna del Alabardero €€

This restaurant was originally opened by a Jesuit priest, Fray Luis de Lezama, in the 1970s. He gave poor youths the opportunity to work here as waiters. The building dates back even further – to the 16th century, when it was a townhouse. Situated near the Teatro Real, the restaurant has a cute terrace that attracts the theatre crowd during the summer. Tapas are served in the bar and Basque cuisine in the restaurant.

✉ Calle Felipe V 6
☎ 91 547 2577
🆆 www.grupolezama.es
🕐 Daily 1–4 and 9–midnight
🚇 Ópera

CHUECA AND THE NORTH

Bazaar Restaurant €€

Bazaar is a fashionable restaurant in the heart of the gay district of Chueca. There are plenty of other bars and restaurants nearby, and it's only a 2-minute walk from the nearest metro. The upper floor is vast and has fabulous natural light, thanks to the huge windows, and the basement has a more intimate feel. The food here is beautifully presented.

✉ Calle Libertad 21
☎ 91 523 3905
🆆 www.restaurantbazaar.com
🕐 Mon–Sun 1–4 and 8:30–11:45
🚇 Chueca

Bristol Bar €€–€€€

The Bristol Bar is seriously stylish. It is also famed for its selection of more than 50 gin-based drinks. The bar has a buzzing atmosphere; the restaurant is more serene, fashionably decorated in striking red and black with an enormous chandelier hanging above. The portions here are extremely generous and perfectly presented. Try the duck with orange sauce, served on a bed of fried potatoes.

✉ Calle del Almirante 20
☎ 91 522 4568
🆆 www.bristolbar.es
🕐 Mon–Wed 9am–midnight, Thu–Fri 9am–1am, Sat 11am–1.30am
🚇 Chueca

Café Oliver €€

This restaurant is popular for its Sunday brunch. The style is bare brick and painted walls, with aged wooden beams and large mirrors. Steak tartare is the signature dish, but there is also some excellent pasta and risotto on offer.

✉ Calle Almirante 12
☎ 91 521 7379
🆆 www.cafeoliver.com
🕐 Sun–Thu 1:30–4 and 9pm–midnight (also Sun brunch 11:30–4), Fri–Sat 1:30–4 and 9pm–1am; closed Aug Sun–Mon
🚇 Chueca

Cocina del Desierto €€

This is a great little Aladdin's cave-type place where people sit on cushions and dine at low tables in true Moroccan style. The walls are whitewashed and there's Moroccan paraphernalia all over the place: trumpets hang above the bar, lamps give off a cosy glow and African music completes the set up. Even the waiters are in traditional African dress. The food is Moroccan and full of exotic flavour. Don't miss the mint tea after your meal.

✉ Calle Barbieri 1
☎ 91 523 1142
🕐 Mon–Fri 1:30–4 and 9–midnight, Sat–Sun 1:30–4:30 and 9–12:30
🚇 Chueca

Dolce Piazzetta €

This is an ice-cream parlour specialising in frozen desserts. There are fresh sorbets bursting with tangy citrus flavours and a variety of ice creams. The terrace is on the main square in the district of Chueca, and it's a perfect place to chill out in the heat and engage in some people watching.

✉ Plaza de Chueca 5
☎ 91 523 8992

🕐 Tue–Fri noon–1am and Sat noon–2am, Sun noon–4pm
🚇 Chueca

Kikuyu €€€
The name of this restaurant comes from an African tribe, but the food is Mediterranean-based, with rice as a speciality. Many dishes exhibit an innovative fusion of flavours and the menu is constantly updated with new touches. The décor is a little stark and in need of an update, but the service and quality of the food do more than compensate. Kikuyu is popular with local business people and the up-market crowd.
✉ Calle Bárbara de Braganza 4
☎ 91 319 6611
🌐 www.kikuyu.es
🕐 Mon–Sat 1:30–3:45 and 9–midnight, closed public hols
🚇 Chueca or Alonso Martínez

Kim Bu Mbu €€
This African restaurant has really cool décor, including the three carved statues and tables that look like treasure chests. The papaya, avocado and spinach salad seasoned with orange, cumin and spices is a popular favourite, and the unusual ingredients such as yucca make a great change from potatoes. The service is excellent, the decor inventive and modern, and the food faultless.
✉ Calle Colmenares 4
☎ 91 521 2681
🌐 www.kimbumbu.com
🕐 Mon–Thu 1:30–4 and 9–midnight, Fri–Sat 1:30–4:30 and 9pm–12:30am, Sun 1:30–4:30
🚇 Chueca

Mastropiero €
Pizza bases fly through the air in this gem of a restaurant as the skilful chefs toss the dough. There's plenty more to look at as well – antiquated concert posters line the walls and ripped sheets of butcher's paper are used instead of plates. They serve Argentinean pizza, the most authentic of which is topped with mozzarella and Roquefort cheeses, caramelised onion, celery salt and walnuts. Pizza slices are available to take away for as little as €3. Don't miss the free slice of chocolate cake at the end of your meal.
✉ Calle de San Vicente Ferrer 34
🕐 Mon–Thu and Sun 8pm–11:45pm, Fri–Sat 8pm–1:45am
🚇 Tribunal or Noviciado

Nabucco €
Situated on the fringes of Madrid's gay district, Nabucco offers the unusual combination of Italian-opera-singing waiters and fresh pizza. The decor is as quirky as the service, with a Roman theme running through the dining room and a glittering chunk of amethyst sitting in the corner. Don't miss the other treats on the menu either, such as the "crepes", which are actually courgette omelettes filled with Brie.
✉ Calle Hortaleza 108
☎ 91 310 0611
🌐 www.nabuccorestaurante.com
🕐 Mon–Fri 1:30–4 and 8:30–midnight, Sat–Sun 1:30–4 and 8:30pm–1am
🚇 Alonso Martínez or Tribunal

Ottocento €€
This Italian-Argentinean restaurant is located in the lively Chueca district, with lots of bars nearby. It occupies the location that the now-defunct Carmencita restaurant inhabited for 150 years. The bright blue walls give a young and vibrant feel that is in keeping with the surroundings, and the elegant chandeliers and antiques add a touch of class. A midday set menu is available for just under €10. The risotto is a popular dish among regulars.
✉ Calle Libertad 16
☎ 91 521 6904
🌐 www.ottocento.es
🕐 Daily 1:30–4, 9–1am
🚇 Chueca

Shopping

Not so very long ago Madrid was most definitely a shopping backwater. You might have come here for museums or nightlife, but not for the shopping. Things have changed hugely in the last couple of decades. Designer names have landed and carved out their niche here, as have high street fashion names such as Zara. There are also a great many small, independent shops selling a huge range of quirky things that you can't find in the chain stores.

CENTRO

Boo-Yaa

This trendy second-hand shop is in the centre of Madrid's bohemian Chueca district. The prices are reasonable and it's hard to tell that the clothes aren't brand new. The shop draws in a young and hip clientele.

- ✉ Calle Hortaleza 3
- ☎ 91 523 4535
- Ⓜ Gran Vía

Casa del Libro

This is an enormous and popular bookshop located slam-bang in Madrid's busiest shopping street. There's a comprehensive stock of Spanish books on every subject, and also a section of English books and teaching aids.

- ✉ Calle Gran Vía 29
- ☎ 902 026402
- ⓦ www.casadellibro.com
- Ⓜ Gran Vía

El Corte Inglés

Most Spanish people's one-stop solution to all their shopping problems, El Corte Inglés is Spain's largest retail concern, with several branches in most larger cities (over 20 in Madrid alone) and at least one in most provincial capitals. You can get practically anything here – clothes, sportswear and equipment, household goods, books and multimedia products. There is also a range of services such as a travel agency and ticket counter for big events.

- ✉ Calle Preciados 1–4
- ☎ 90 112 2122 (for all branches)
- ⓦ www.elcorteingles.es
- Ⓜ Sol

Custo

This is one of two Custo shops in Madrid – the other is on Calle Mayor. The designs by this Catalan designer are bold, bright and original. There's a wide range of t-shirts and also dresses, skirts and jackets. Prices aren't cheap, but quality is high.

- ✉ Calle Fuencarral 29
- ☎ 91 360 4636
- ⓦ www.custo-barcelona.com
- Ⓜ Gran Vía or Chueca

FNAC

This French chain is a one-stop solution for books (including foreign-language publications), music, DVDs and a huge range of electronic products, generally at very competitive prices. Fnac also sells tickets for concerts, and offers a reading room and newspaper store with foreign newspapers and magazines.

- ✉ Calle Preciados 28
- ☎ 91 595 6200
- ⓦ www.fnac.es
- Ⓜ Callao

Kwaleon

This branch is just one of a number of these cool and über-funky men's shops, packed full of skating and boarding clothes.

✉ Gran Vía 51
☎ 91 559 7542
Ⓜ Sol

Librería San Ginés

This is a quaint bookshop that's not really a shop, as it's situated outside in a narrow passageway near the San Ginés chocolateriá. It sells everything from old English paperbacks to limited editions. It pays to spend time rooting through the chaos.

✉ Pasadizo de San Ginés 2
☎ 91 366 4686
Ⓜ Sol

Nike

This is a sports fan's heaven. This spacious store stocks t-shirts, tracksuits and all the usual sporting paraphernalia. It's located on one of the busiest streets in the city and there are plenty of other shops, bars and restaurants nearby.

✉ Calle Gran Vía 38
☎ 91 523 7358
Ⓜ Gran Vía

Piedra de Luna

This shop is like a treasure trove of worldly items. Expect to find kilims and ceramics from Morocco, Indian jewellery and authentic wooden furniture. The shop has a hippy, yet cosy feel.

✉ Calle Príncipe 14
☎ 91 521 6373
Ⓜ Sevilla

Rastro

No shopping trip to Madrid would be complete without a visit to the city's oldest flea market, El Rastro. Nowadays it's a bit of a tourist trap, but bargains can still be found. Everything is on offer from cushions and throws to CDs and house plants.

Branching off the main drag, the Ribera de Curtidores, are many smaller streets where cheaper goods are for sale.

✉ Calle de la Ribera de Curtidores
Ⓜ La Latina

Trendy Tube

A funky shop providing a link to London fashion – the blouses here are much sought after. Also look at the "shirts in a can", which are t-shirts printed with bold designs that come served in a can! The owner is bilingual, so shopping here is easy for non-Spanish speakers.

✉ Corredera Baja de San Pablo 46
☎ 91 523 8873
Ⓜ Callao or Gran Vía

Zara

Zara is a hugely popular Spanish high-street clothing store with functional and up-to-date designs at fair prices. There are clothes for women, men and children. Zara has branches all over Madrid and elsewhere in Spain, as well as in many other countries.

✉ Gran Vía 30
☎ 91 521 1283
Ⓜ Gran Vía

JERÓNIMOS AND THE EAST

Carolina Herrera

This is a famous and sophisticated boutique stocking men's and women's clothes. There are also stylish bags, scarves and accessories. The cool and dark interior contrasts with bright and cheerful items, which are all of excellent quality. Blouses start at €170.

✉ Calle Serrano 16
☎ 91 781 4380
ⓦ www.carolinaherrera.com
Ⓜ Serrano

Chucu-Chu

This shop stocks quality handmade clothing for children and teenagers, plus maternity clothing. It's in the elegant Salamanca district and has many other designer boutiques as neighbours.

✉ Calle Príncipe de Vergara 66 and 68
☎ 91 562 2911
Ⓜ Nuñez de Balboa

Diesel

Just one of many branches worldwide of the famous casuals store. Here are top quality street clothes and shoes for a young, hip and trendy crowd. Jackets cost approximately €230 and blouses €100.

✉ Calle Serrano 14
☎ 91 431 3166
Ⓜ Serrano

Farrutx

This is a shoe-shopper's heaven, with gorgeous handmade Spanish footwear. Situated in the elegant district of Salamanca, there are many exclusive designer shops further along the same street. The prices match the high quality.

✉ Calle Serrano 7
☎ 91 576 9493
Ⓦ www.farrutx.com
Ⓜ Retiro

Gallery

This is a shop for men who like style. Meterosexuals will love the selection of shoes, bags, belts, CDs, suits and casual wear. Shoppers can rehydrate themselves at the trendy mineral-water bar.

✉ Calle de Jorge Juan 38
☎ 91 576 7931
Ⓦ www.gallerymadrid.com
Ⓜ Príncipe de Vergara

Hermès

This shop is found in the upmarket district of Salamanca. It started as a place to buy horse-riding gear, but has since expanded to include a range of men's and women's clothing. They have an exquisite selection of ties and handkerchiefs.

✉ Calle José Ortega y Gasset 12
☎ 91 578 3041

Ⓦ www.hermes.com
Ⓜ Nuñez de Balboa

Hoss Intropia

A boutique for the well-to-do shopper who wants colourful and floaty attire. They stock clothes for all occasions and prices start at around €60 for a blouse.

✉ Calle Serrano 18
☎ 91 781 0612
Ⓦ www.hossintropia.com
Ⓜ Serrano

Jardín de Serrano

This is a small, but classy shopping centre with designer boutiques and an elegant café where the upper classes sip lattes and watch the world go by.

✉ Calle Goya 6-8
☎ 91 577 0012
Ⓦ www.jardindeserrano.es
Ⓜ Serrano

Javier Simorra

This designer shop stocks pricey clothes for young and vibrant people. Jeans and sweaters start at €100. The skirts are very feminine and the general style is fresh.

✉ Calle Serrano 33
☎ 91 576 8699
Ⓦ www.simorra.com
Ⓜ Serrano

Lavinia

This is a bright, spacious and airy wine shop, far removed from a traditional Spanish bodega. The staff are very helpful and knowledgeable. There's an elegant restaurant which offers a variety of meat and fish dishes.

✉ Calle José Ortega y Gasset 16
☎ 91 426 0604
Ⓦ www.lavinia.com
Ⓜ Nuñez de Balboa

Marina Rinaldi

This designer boutique caters to the well-heeled client. Blouses are priced around

€300 and trousers at €140. The clothes are more "outdoor" as opposed to "city", and the style is smart and casual.

✉ Calle Serrano 38
☎ 91 436 0230
Ⓜ Serrano

Vinçon

This shop is an emporium of design, located inside an old red-brick factory. It sells bathroom fixtures, accessories, cutlery, lighting and other household items.

✉ Calle de Castelló 18
☎ 91 578 0520
🔤 www.vincon.com
Ⓜ Velázquez

PALACIO AND THE WEST

Centro Comercial Príncipe Pío

This grand shopping centre to the southwest of the city centre is built inside an old railway station. In addition to two floors of high-street shops, there are bars and restaurants that spill on to outdoor terraces in the summer. There's also a cinema showing films dubbed in Spanish.

✉ Paseo de la Florida 2
🔤 www.ccprincipepio.com
Ⓜ Príncipe Pío

El Flamenco Vive

This is a wonderful shop, chock-full of flamenco paraphernalia. There's everything from CDs to guitars, books and clothing. It's a great place for tourists, to buy souvenirs but it's also got everything that a true flamenco aficionado could want.

✉ Calle Conde de Lemos 7
☎ 91 547 3917
🔤 www.elflamencovive.es
Ⓜ Ópera

Marre Moerel Design Studio

A shop full of original lighting and tableware in limited editions by Dutch designer Marre Moerel. They also do shipments to overseas addresses.

✉ Calle de Noviciado 4
☎ 91 523 9059
🔤 www.marremoerel.com
Ⓜ Noviciado

CHUECA AND THE NORTH

Ama Records

A cool "alternative" record store located inside the Mercado (market) de Fuencarral. It stocks acid, jazz, drum and bass, hip-hop and a range of imported material.

✉ San Lorenzo 19
☎ 91 310 4616
🔤 www.ama-records.com
Ⓜ Tribunal

El Apartamento

This furniture shop prides itself on offering retro furniture and accessories from the 1950s, '60s and '70s. There's even wallpaper for sale, and every other imaginable household object. The shop takes its name from the Billy Wilder film.

✉ Calle Ruíz 11
☎ 91 445 7768
🔤 www.elapartamento.biz
Ⓜ Bilbao

Caligae

Calle Augusto Figueroa is where the girls can shop for more hip and unusual styles than otherwise found on the high street. This one is a shoe shop that offers great discounts on designer names.

✉ Calle Augusto Figueroa 20
☎ 91 531 6537
Ⓜ Chueca

Desigual

Some say this is the poorer cousin of Custo, as the designs are equally as bright and eye-catching. Desigual attracts a younger crowd, though, and the prices are much more affordable. The branch on calle Mayor is open on Sundays.

✉ Calle de Fuencarral 36
☎ 90 213 3138

www.desigual.com
Tribunal or Gran Vía

Glam

Glam is one of the pioneer fashion shops in Fuencarral. They sell their own original designs and also local and international brands. Glam shoes is now open next door, with some of the trendiest trainers in town.

Calle Fuencarral 35
91 532 1114
www.glam.es
Tribunal

HAND

This is a randomly stocked shop that sells French designer-label clothing and items brought back from the owner's travels in India! HAND is short for "Have A Nice Day". It's quite surreal, but worth a look just for the experience.

Calle Hortaleza 26
91 521 5152
www.hand-haveaniceday.es
Chueca

Hespen & Suárez

This is not a place to visit for people on a diet. American Kay Hespen and her Spanish husband José Suárez started out in the catering business and became so successful that they branched out into retail. They now stock wines, nougat, takeaway dishes and jams.

Calle Barceló 15
91 445 3903
www.hespenysuarez.com
Tribunal or Alonso Martínez

Isolée

This shop is like an Aladdin's cave of clothes, accessories, food and homeware. Everything is individually chosen to appeal to the well-heeled jet-setter. There are both national and international designer labels, including RED Valentino. Customers can also download tunes onto their iPods and visit the downstairs bar for a drink.

Calle de las Infantas 19
902 876136
www.isolee.com
Chueca

J&J Books and Coffee

This great little coffee bar and bookstore is a good place to meet people. The ground floor is warm and inviting, and the basement stocks a large selection of English-language books. The café holds "open mike" nights, as well as foreign exchange evenings.

Calle del Espíritu Santo 47
91 521 8576
www.jandjbooksandcoffee.com
Noviciado

Loreak Mendian

An affordable and funky shop for men with exclusive designs that are unique to Spain. The clothes are way ahead of the high-street fashions and it is a great place for finding original and distinctive items.

Calle de Santa Barbára 4
91 522 2865
www.loreakmendian.com
Alonso Martínez

Maison Blanche

This is a super-cool luxury food store in the Chueca district. The design of the shop is minimalist and the products are sumptuous. The wonderful deli sells tasty morsels from around the world.

Calle de Piamonte 10
91 522 8217
Chueca

Mercado de Fuencarral

The coolest people shop for authentic bohemian styles in this indoor market. There are three floors of hippy and funky clothes, jewellery stores, tattoo parlours and a cinema and concert space.

Calle de Fuencarral 45
91 521 4152
Tribunal

Entertainment

Madrid has long enjoyed a reputation as a "fun" city with all manner of entertainments to suit all tastes, both highbrow and less so. The night scene is legendary, having made headlines worldwide during the heady days of the "movida" in the mid 1980s. Things have calmed down a little since then, and the city authorities have become a lot stricter on opening hours and partying on the streets, but there is still plenty of fun to be had for those who really want it, which is not surprising for a city which supposedly has more bars in a 1-kilometre radius of the Puerta del Sol than the whole of Norway and Sweden put together.

CENTRO

La Boca del Lobo
People love this small bar because of its eclectic music, which ranges from rock, funk, electronic jazz and rare grooves to R&B and African. There are also live gigs.
✉ Calle Echegaray 11
☎ 91 429 7013
🆆 www.labocadellobo.com
🚇 Sevilla

Café de Chinitas
An authentic and popular restaurant plus flamenco show, with lots of famous Spanish folk artists performing regularly. The guest list has included the King of Spain, Lady Diana and Bill Clinton.
✉ Calle Torija 7

☎ 91 559 5135
🆆 www.chinitas.com
🚇 Santo Domingo

Café de Círculo de Bellas Artes
This café is grand and stately, with larger-than-life nude statues, huge frescos and old-fashioned waiters in penguin suits. More than just a café, the rest of the building hosts exhibitions and concerts on a regular basis. A magnet for the arty set.
✉ Calle Marqués de Casa Riera 2
☎ 91 521 6942
🆆 www.circulobellasartes.com
🚇 Banco de España

Café de los Austrias
This is a traditional-style café with a simple charm, sited close to the Palacio Real in

the most charming area of the city. It sits alongside a picturesque square where chairs and tables are available outside in summer. The restaurant serves simple and authentic Spanish dishes, such as potato croquettes and Spanish omelette.

✉ Plaza de Ramales 1
☎ 91 559 8436
🌐 www.cafedelosaustrias.com
Ⓜ Ópera

Casa Patas

This is a great place to watch excellent flamenco dancing and singing. The shows book up fast, so reservations are necessary. The brightly lit restaurant serves a filling meal before the show, or there's the option to skip dinner and just view the performance. The audience here is made up of serious flamenco buffs.

✉ Calle Cañizares 10
☎ 91 369 0496
🌐 www.casapatas.com
Ⓜ Tirso de Molina or Antón Martín

Chocolatería San Ginés

Situated next to the old church of the same name, this place is a veritable institution – it has been open for over 100 years. The speciality is thick hot chocolate served with churros, which are fried sticks of dough. Madrileños usually enjoy them for breakfast after a night out dancing, or at around 6pm. However, San Ginés is now so popular that hot chocolate flows almost 24 hours a day.

✉ Pasadizo de San Ginés 5
☎ 91 365 6546
Ⓜ Sol

Delic

This bar has a reputation as one of the funkiest and most chilled out places in the district of La Latina. The aroma of their superb mojitos floats out into the adjacent square, where customers sit on the bar's terrace beneath shady trees. The interior is decked out in retro style. It's always packed to the gills with a laid-back arty crowd.

✉ Costanilla de San Andrés 14
☎ 91 364 5450
🌐 www.deliccafe.com
Ⓜ La Latina

Joy Eslava

Joy is a nightclub situated in what used to be a theatre. It has a sumptuous feel that is popular with locals and tourists alike. The club hosts gigs as well as dance nights. Expect to be painting the town red alongside models, actors and singers on the dance floor.

✉ Calle Arenal 11
☎ 91 366 3733
🌐 www.joy-eslava.com
Ⓜ Sol or Ópera

Kapital

This seven-floor mega club throws glitz and glamour straight in your face. The music includes everything from house to hip-hop to Spanish pop. The dress code allows for anything except trainers. The club is popular with both tourists and Madrid residents.

✉ Calle Atocha 125
☎ 91 429 1665, 91 420 2906
🌐 www.grupo-kapital.com
Ⓜ Atocha

Marula Café

Just under the magnificent viaduct over the Calle de Segovia, this is the funkiest nightclub in La Latina, with jam sessions every Monday. The interior space is pretty small, but the atmosphere is bohemian and relaxed. Cool music includes funk, soul and groove. In the summer, people spill out on to the street, where they start the evening sipping drinks on the terrace.

✉ Calle de Caños de los Viejos 3
☎ 91 366 1596
🌐 www.marulacafe.com
Ⓜ La Latina

Museo Chicote

This trendy city-centre bar won the "Best European Bar 2004" award given by MTV-

Campari. Many a famous celebrity worth a mention has sipped cocktails here, including Ava Gardner, Frank Sinatra, Lana Turner, Gary Cooper, Orson Wells, Yul Brynner, Ernest Hemingway – and more recently – Catherine Zeta Jones, Hugh Grant and Tim Robbins. The decor is exactly as it was when the bar first opened in the 1930s and they serve some of the best cocktails in town.

✉ Calle Gran Vía 12
☎ 91 532 6737
ⓦ www.museo-chicote.com
Ⓜ Gran Vía

Palacio Gaviria

This nightclub was formerly a palace constructed in 1846, inspired by Italian Renaissance style. Its massive interior has 13 stately rooms decked out in a plush and regal fashion. There are three DJs playing simultaneously and the music includes everything from Latin beats to house and pop.

✉ Calle Arenal 9
☎ 91 526 6069, 91 526 6070
ⓦ www.palaciogaviria.com
Ⓜ Ópera or Sol

Tablao las Carboneras

Carboneras is a small and intimate flamenco bar and restaurant with a fantastic ambience. It's run by three dancers who have put their souls into every aspect of the place. The restaurant serves hearty Spanish food. There are two shows per night, guaranteed to leave your heart pounding in your chest.

✉ Plaza del Conde de Miranda 1
☎ 91 542 8677
ⓦ www.tablaolascarboneras.com
Ⓜ Sol

Las Tablas

This is a small, but sophisticated flamenco venue directed by Antonia Moya and Marisol Navarro, two experienced dancers from the flamenco world. The emphasis is on quality flamenco performances and the atmosphere is intense. Different artists play each night – the show begins at 10.30pm and goes on for 75 minutes.

✉ Plaza de España 9, corner Cuesta de San Vicente
☎ 91 542 0520
ⓦ www.lastablasmadrid.com
Ⓜ Plaza de España

Torres Bermejas

The decor of this flamenco bar is designed to resemble the Alhambra in Granada, giving it a real Andalusian feel. There is a large group of dancers here who perform flamenco and classical Spanish dancing. The restaurant offers a choice of three tasty menus.

✉ Calle de Mesonero Romanos 11
☎ 91 532 3322
ⓦ www.torresbermejas.com
Ⓜ Gran Vía

El Viajero

The highlight of this three-storey bar and restaurant is its roof terrace. El Viajero is the perfect place to begin an evening out as it sits at the end of the well known Cava Baja street, which is packed full of bars. The atmosphere is buzzing and the cocktails are very popular.

✉ Plaza de la Cebada 11
☎ 91 366 9064
Ⓜ La Latina

JERÓNIMOS AND THE EAST

Florida Park

This venue in Parque del Retiro was previously a royal hunting pavilion, chapel and spa before it was transformed into an elegant nightclub and restaurant. The elite come to Florida Park to watch Spanish ballet and flamenco, and to dance on the nights when there are DJs. Enter from Calle Menéndez Pelayo, opposite Calle Ibiza.

✉ Paseo República de Panamá 1
☎ 91 573 7805

www.floridapark.net

Ibiza

PALACIO AND THE WEST

Copolaclub

This is a funky two-storey disco bar with jazz, soul, pop and chill house upstairs, and electronica and techno downstairs. The atmosphere upstairs is relaxed and chatty, while downstairs is for dance fiends only. The public get to test out their DJ-ing skills on weeknights. Worth a visit just to get a drink in one of the enormous glasses.

Calle San Hermenegildo 7

68 754 7285

www.copolaclub.com

San Bernardo or Noviciado

Corral de la Morería

This flamenco tablao has been going since 1956. During its heyday, many famous artists from the flamenco world graced the stage – namely Blanca del Rey, Antonio Gades, "La Chunga", Isabel Pantoja and Los del Río. The intimate atmosphere means the audience can soak up the passion of the show. They serve dinner before the show, or there's the option to go only to see the performance. The Corral de la Morería is in a great location, near many other bars in the old quarter of the city.

Calle Morería 17

91 365 8446, 91 365 1137

www.corraldelamoreria.com

Ópera or La Latina

CHUECA AND THE NORTH

Areia

This is a welcoming chill-out bar with cushions scattered along the floor and a four-poster bed at one end. The colours are deep and sumptuous; Moroccan lamps add a subtle glow of light. The music is house, Brazilian beats and minimal. Cocktails are popular at night; during the day, there's the delicious and innovative food to enjoy.

Calle Hortaleza 92

91 310 0307

www.areiachillout.com

Chueca or Alonso Martínez

Café Acuarela

Situated just off the main square in Chueca, Madrid's gay district, this bar has a dark appeal. It's decorated in a camp style with Virgin Mary statues and angels, among other oddities. The overall effect is strangely cosy and welcoming, and most people visit this bar for an intimate chat with friends, to drink tea in the afternoons and caipirinhas at night.

Calle Gravina 10

91 522 2143

Chueca

Pachá

Housed in the old Barceló cinema, Pachá has always been a famous place for fun in Madrid. The building, one of the greatest achievements in architecture in Madrid, was built in 1930 by the award-winning architect Gutiérrez Soto. The decor today is preserved in the original style, giving the club a plush feel. Pachá is hugely popular with dance music lovers. The dress code is quite daring.

Calle Barceló 11

91 447 0128

www.pacha-madrid.com

Tribunal

Sala Clamores

Situated close to grungy Malasaña, but really close to the lovely Plaza Olavide, this sala specialises in offering jazz, blues, ethnic, Caribbean, afro, tango and flamenco music. Artists who have played here include Joe Henderson and Dave Murray. It also plays host to an English-language comedy show once a month in the winter.

Calle Alburquerque 14

91 445 7938

www.salaclamores.com

Bilbao

Travel Facts

Madrid has something for everyone, from serious art buffs to incorrigible night-owls, from gastronomes to theatre lovers. Here are some pointers about the practical aspects that will be important to making your stay in this exciting, vibrant city comfortable and enjoyable, from arrival to getting around, and from advice on currency to climate, driving and health care, and much more besides.

ARRIVING

Formalities for EU members

Anyone entering Spain must have a valid passport or for EU nationals, their national ID card. Visa requirements are subject to change so check before you travel. Passengers on flights to Spain (since 2007) must produce Advance Passenger Information. Check with your travel agent before travelling.

Visitors from outside the EU

All non-EU citizens must produce a full passport, though travellers from the US, Canada, Australia, New Zealand, Japan and Israel, as well as other countries with which Spain has special agreements do not need a visa for stays shorter than 90 days. Visitors from other countries need a visa before travelling and should apply at the Spanish consulate nearest their place of residence.

Airport

Madrid's Barajas Airport is 13km (8 miles) to the northeast of the city. Many major airlines, including **one**world members such as British Airways, Iberia and American Airways, use the new T4 terminal. Budget airlines such as easyJet and Ryanair and Aer Lingus arrive at T1. Some domestic flights and other Spanish airlines arriving from Schengen countries use T3, while other local flights and the Barcelona shuttle use T2. The metro (underground) stations Aeropuerto T1-T2-T3 and Aeropuerto T4 (both on line 8) serve the corresponding terminals. There is a €1 airport supplement on top of the ticket price. The airport line terminates at Nuevos Ministerios station.

Arriving by Train

Trains from France and the north of Spain arrive at Chamartín station, in the north of the city. Those from southern, western and eastern points and from Portugal arrive at Atocha, south of the city centre.

Madrid now has high-speed links to several other Spanish cities. Trains leave Atocha for Toledo, Sevilla, Cordoba and Malaga in the south and Zaragoza, Lleida, Tarragona and Barcelona to the east. Chamartín handles services to and from Segovia and Valladolid, to the north.

The Chamartín and Atocha stations are connected by an underground main line rail link that is currently being duplicated, with a link to Puerta del Sol, in the centre of Madrid. Both have good metro and bus links to central Madrid as well as local trains (the Cercanía network) to many points throughout the Madrid region. Exchange facilities and tourist information are available at both stations.

Other Options

Travellers coming by coach bus from Spain and abroad arrive mostly at the main Estación del Sur bus station, at the Méndez Álvaro metro station or the Continental Auto station on Avenida de América.

CALENDAR OF EVENTS

January
Noche de Reyes (Kings' Night or Epiphany): on the night of 5 January, thousands of families line the streets to watch the annual parade with the Three Kings, who throw sweets to the children from their floats. The following day, Reyes, is a family festival where presents are given to the children.

January/February
Carnaval (Carnival): Many Madrileños dress up and party during carnival week. Ash Wednesday sees the "burial of the sardine", a wacky ceremony to mark the end of the carnival week.

March
Semana Santa (Easter): Holy Week falls in late March or early April. Look out

for parish processions in which figures of Christ and the Virgin are carried around by hooded penitents.

April
Madrid en Danza: Madrid's annual international festival of dance is held across several venues throughout the city.

May
Dos de Mayo: May 2 is when the city commemorates the uprising of the people of Madrid against the occupying Napoleonic troops in 1808.

May/June
Feria del Libro: Madrid's major book fair takes place in the Parque del Retiro (Retiro park) – and is usually accompanied by a downpour after weeks of splendid spring weather!

May/July
PhotoEspaña: a huge photographic jamboree involving dozens of exhibitions in museums, art galleries and public spaces.

June
San Antonio de la Florida: The feast day of San Antonio falls on 13 June and celebrates the patron saint of seamstresses, among other things. A big street party is held on this day, close to the hermitage named for the saint.

July/August
Veranos de la Villa (Summer in the City): This summer festival comprises outdoor theatre, cinema, music, opera and zarzuelas (a Spanish form of operetta) at several venues throughout the city.

August
Verbenas de San Cayetano, San Lorenzo and Paloma: These are various street parties held in the old central neighbourhoods of Lavapiés, Rastro and La Latina.

September
Noche en Blanco: One for insomniacs, this event sees galleries, museums and other exhibition spaces staying open all night. Entry is free at this time.

October/November
Festival de Otoño: Madrid's five-week long Autumn Festival is the city's main performing arts event. It draws together a vast range of acts, troupes and companies from all over the world.

December
Navidad (Christmas): The city is beautifully illuminated from late November onwards and there is a fun Christmas market in the Plaza Mayor throughout December.

New Year's Eve: The New Year is greeted with great relish. Crowds gather in the Puerta del Sol to celebrate by stuffing twelve grapes in their mouths, in time to the chimes of the clock.

CLIMATE
Madrid's climate, the popular saying goes, is "tres meses de infierno, y nueve meses de invierno" (three months of hell and nine months of winter). Summers are mightily hot – mid-afternoon temperatures often climb above 40ºC (104ºF) in July and August, with little respite at night. Spring and autumn are fairly short, but bring much-welcome rain and can also be pleasantly warm, allowing for eating and drinking outdoors. Winter can be very cold; but even then, in January and February, there are crisp but sunny days with glorious blue skies.

CLOTHING
In summer, light, loose-fitting cotton clothes are essential and sandals, headgear and sunglasses are recommended. In winter, a sweater or fleece pullover plus a warm jacket or coat are needed. In spring and autumn, though it can get quite hot at times, a jacket and a sweater or fleece are

never amiss. Smart casual is acceptable attire almost anywhere.

CUSTOMS

When arriving from other EU countries, EU citizens do not have to declare goods imported from those countries, provided tax has been paid when purchasing them. Customs officers may question if large amounts of any item are genuinely for the traveller's personal use. Random spot checks are carried out for drugs.

You can bring 800 cigarettes or 200 cigars. 10L (0.2 gallons) of spirits (over 22% alcohol) or 20L (0.4 gallons) of fortified wine or alcoholic drinks with less than 22% alcohol is allowed.

For non-EU residents, or from outside the EU, you can bring up to 200 cigarettes, 50 cigars or 250g (9 ounces) of loose tobacco. 1L (0.02 gallons) of spirits (over 22% alcohol) or 2L (0.04 gallons) of any other alcoholic beverage with less than 22% alcohol content is allowed.

Within reasonable limits, there are no restrictions on cameras, watches or electrical goods, and visitors can also carry up to €6,000 in cash. When leaving, non-EU residents may claim back the VAT (Value Added Tax) paid on purchases of over €90.15 in value. Go to the Global Refund Office at Barajas airport and look out for the Tax Free sticker in the window of outlets.

DRIVING

Owing to the traffic saturation, driving around Madrid is rarely easy. The city has excellent public transport, though, so it is much simpler to get around on the metro and buses. If you do drive, bear in mind that Spanish road regulations are basically in line with those in force throughout the EU regarding the use of seat belts and the obligation to carry warning triangles and spare parts. You can drive with a valid driving licence from most countries and should keep all documents with you at all times, or you may be fined. Do not leave

any valuables or important documents in a parked car. Foreign-registered cars are likely targets for car thieves.

Car Rental

Renting a vehicle can be expensive, so it is best to shop around – cheap deals are available especially on weekends. All hire companies have a minimum age requirement, usually 21, and you should have held a full licence for at least a year. All major companies operate in Madrid. Check the websites of the main ones, such as www.avis.es, www.easycar.es, www.europcar.es or www.hertz.es.

ELECTRICITY

Most buildings in Spain now have 230-volt circuits, though very old and rural hotels and *pensiones* may still have the old 125-volt installed, which would mean using a transformer. Check before using any electrical appliances. As Spanish plugs are of the two-pin variety, an adaptor is necessary to use any electrical appliances brought from the UK.

EMBASSIES AND CONSULATES

Australia: Plaza del Descubridor Diego de Ordás 3
Tel: 91 353 6600;
www.spain.embassy.gov.au
Canada: Calle Núñez de Balboa 35
Tel: 91 423 3250;
www.canada-es.org
France: Calle de Salustiano Olózaga 9
Tel: 91 423 8900;
www.ambafrance-es.org
Germany: Calle Fortuny 8
Tel: 91 557 9000;
www.madrid.diplo.de
Ireland: Paseo de la Castellana 46, 4º
Tel: 91 576 3500
Japan: Calle Serrano 109
Tel: 91 590 7600;
www.es.emb-japan.go.jp
Netherlands: Avenida Comandante Franco 32

Tel: 91 353 7500;
www.emajadapaisesbajos.es
New Zealand: Plaza de la Lealtad 2 3°
Tel: 91 523 0226;
www.nzembassy.com
South Africa: Edificio Lista, Calle Claudio
Coello 91
Tel: 91 436 3789;
www.sudafrica.com
UK: Calle de Fernando el Santo 16
Tel: 91 700 8200, 91 524 9700;
www.ukinspain.com
USA: Calle Serrano 75
Tel: 91 587 2200;
www.embusa.es

EMERGENCY TELEPHONE NUMBERS

The general free number for emergency
services is 112. Some attendants may
speak English or another European
language such as French or German. If you
wish to call the police directly, the number
for the Policía Municipal is 092; for the
Policía Nacional dial 091.

GETTING AROUND

Madrid's public transport system is good
and reasonably cheap, and has been
greatly improved in recent years.

Short-stay visitors can save money with
two ticket types. The ten-ride Metrobus, for
use on either the metro or buses, costs less
than 70 per cent of the price of 10 single
rides. Each time you get on a bus or enter
the metro, you must validate the ticket.
Alternatively, the Tourist Travel Pass *(Abono
Turístico)* offers unlimited use of metro,
buses and local trains for 1, 2, 3, 5 or 7
days. You can buy either ticket at any metro
station or many tobacconists' *(estancos)*.

HEALTH FACILITIES

For EU citizens, Form E111 is no longer
valid and has been replaced by the
European Health Insurance Card (EHIC),
which should be obtained before travelling.
The EHIC is not a substitute for medical
and travel insurance, but does give

entitlement to emergency medical treatment
on the same terms as Spanish nationals.
It does not cover medical repatriation, or
on-going or non-urgent medical treatment.

Non-EU citizens should take out
comprehensive travel and health insurance
before travelling to Spain.

LANGUAGE

Spain's principal language is Spanish, also
known as Castilian (Castellano), and some
knowledge of it is useful as English is not
very widely spoken, though this is slowly
changing.

MONEY MATTERS

Spain joined the Eurozone in 2002. A euro
consists of 100 cents (céntimos), with
coins of 1, 2, 5 10, 20 and 50 cents as
well as €1 and €2 coins. Notes come in
different coloured denominations of €5,
€10, €20, €50, €100, €200 and €500. You
can change money or travellers' cheques in
most city-centre banks and savings banks
(cajas de ahorro) or at bureaux de change
– look for the cambio sign. Have valid ID
with you. Remember, you are likely to get
a better rate at a bank. Commission rates
vary, but it may be cheaper to take money
out of an ATM with a credit or debit card.
American Express has seven offices at
Barajas airport, four in T-4, three in T-1 and
two in T-2.

OPENING HOURS

Banks usually open Mon–Fri 8:30–2. Some banks, especially savings banks (*cajas de ahorro*) also have extended hours once a week, usually on Thursday afternoon/early evening; others stay open until 4pm on Fridays or open on Saturdays 9–1. From the first working day in May to the last in September, most banks do not have extended hours however.

Shops and Department Stores

There has been considerable liberalisation of opening hours in Madrid in recent years. Timings for most small shops are approximately 10–2 and 5–8/8:30 on weekdays, closing on Saturday afternoons and Sundays. However, supermarkets, hypermarkets and department stores generally stay open all day, from 10–9 or even 10–10, as well as on the first Sunday of every month. Bakeries also open on Sundays, as do shops selling "cultural goods" such as books, CDs and DVDs. In the central area around the Puerta del Sol, any shop can stay open every Sunday of the year, though not all bother.

Government Offices

With three tiers of government in Madrid – central, regional and municipal – opening hours may vary depending on the institution and its functions. Generally speaking, government institutions are open around 9am to 2pm.

POSTAL SERVICES

The easiest way of buying stamps for letters or postcards is to go to a tobacconists' shop *(estanco)*, easily identified by the brown and yellow sign with the word *tobacos*.

SECURITY

Madrid is not an especially dangerous city, but caution and common sense should be exercised, especially at night in central areas such as around Sol and Gran Vía. The Lavapiés neighbourhood has become known as a mugging black spot and the Retiro, the Parque del Oeste and quiet backstreets are best avoided after dark. Pickpocketing and bag-snatching is a problem, especially on buses and the metro; violent crime is less frequent.

TELEPHONE NUMBERS AND CODES

All Madrid numbers begin with 91 followed by 7 more digits. You must dial this entire sequence of numbers, whether you are calling from within the city or from outside.

Spain's country code is 34, so to call Madrid from abroad dial 00 from the UK or 001 from the US, followed by 34, then 91 and the remainder of the number. When calling out of Spain, dial 00 followed by the country code and then the subscriber's number, omitting the initial 0 from UK numbers.

TIPPING

Tipping is at the customer's discretion and there is no fixed, or expected, percentage. A tip of between 5 and 10 per cent is usually enough in restaurants and a small coin or two usually suffices in a bar (rarely more than 15 or 20 cents if you have had just a drink). Similarly, in taxis, a few small coins suffice – but you might give more or less according to how helpful (or not) the driver has been. Hotel porters, toilet and cinema attendants may also be tipped a small amount.

TOURIST OFFICES

The Centro de Turismo de Madrid run by the Madrid City Council is at Plaza Mayor 27; tel: 91 588 1636; e-mail turismo@munimadrid.es.

Index

Spotlight On Madrid

Acknowledgements

The Automobile Association would like to thank the following photographers, companies and picture libraries for their assistance in the preparation of this book.

Abbreviations for the picture credits are as follows – (t) top; (b) bottom; (c) centre; (l) left; (r) right; (AA) AA World Travel Library.

Front Cover a AA/M Jourdan; Front Cover b AA/M Chaplow; Front Cover c AA/ M Jourdan; Front Cover d AA/M Chaplow; Front Cover e AA/R Strange; Front Cover f AA/R Strange; Front Cover g A/M Jourdan; Front Cover h AA/M Jourdan; Front Cover i AA/J Edmanson; Front Cover j AA/J Edmanson; Front Cover k AA/R Strange; 3 AA/M Chaplow; 4l AA/M Chaplow; 4c Turespaña; 4r Centro de Tourismo de Madrid; 5l AA/R Strange; 5c AA/R Strange; 5r Centro de Tourismo de Madrid; 6/7 AA/M Chaplow; 8/9 Centro de Tourismo de Madrid; 12t AA/M Jourdan; 12bl AA/M Jourdan; 13tl AA/M Jourdan; 13tr AA/R Strange; 13b Centro de Tourismo de Madrid; 14 Centro de Tourismo de Madrid; 15 AA/M Chaplow; 16 (i) Bildarchiv Monheim GmbH/Alamy; 16 (ii) AA/M Chaplow; 16 (iii) AA/R Strange; 16 (iv) AA/R Strange; 16 (v) AA/M Chaplow; 18 Bildarchiv Monheim GmbH/Alamy; 19 AA/M Chaplow; 20 AA/M Jourdan; 21 Centro de Tourismo de Madrid; 22 AA/R Strange; 22/23 Mooch Images/Alamy; 23 AA/R Strange; 24 AA/M Chaplow; 26/27 Bildarchiv Monheim GmbH/Alamy; 28 Turespaña 29 Peter Domotor/Alamy; 30/31 AA/M Chaplow; 31 AA/R Strange; 32 AA/P Enticknap; 33 ???; 34 AA/R Strange; 36 AA/R Strange; 37l Biblioteca y Despacho Morques de Cerralbo; 37r Museo Cerralbo; 38t Museo Cerralbo; 38b Museo Cerralbo 38/39 Museo Cerralbo 39t Museo Cerralbo; 39b Museo Cerralbo; 40 AA/M Jourdan; 42/43 Centro de Tourismo de Madrid; 43 AA/M Jourdan; 44 AA/M Chaplow; 45 AA/M Jourdan; 46 Palacio Real; 47l AA/J Edmanson; 47r AA/M Jourdan; 48 AA/R Strange; 48/49 AA/R Strange; 50 AA/R Strange; 51 AA/M Jourdan; 52/53 AA/M Chaplow; 53 AA/M Chaplow; 54/55 AA/M Chaplow; 56 Philip Augustavo/Alamy; 57 AA/R Strange; 58 AA/M Jourdan; 59 AA/M Chaplow; 60cl Alex Segre/Alamy; 60bl AA/M Chaplow; 60bc Turespaña; 61bl AA/M Chaplow; 62t Alamy; 62b AA/M Chaplow; 63 Derrick Alderman/Alamy; 64 AA/R Strange; 66t AA/M Chaplow; 66b Turespaña; 68 AA/R Strange; 69 AA/M Chaplow; 70/71 AA/M Chaplow; 71 AA/R Strange; 72/73 AA/M Chaplow/ © DACS (Secession Picasso); 73 AA/M Chaplow; 74 Centro de Tourismo de Madrid; 75 AA/R Strange; 76/77 Centro de Tourismo de Madrid; 77 Museo Thyssen Bornemisza; 78 AA/M Chaplow; 78/79 brainspain/Alamy; 79 AA/M Jourdan; 80t IML Image Group Ltd; Alamy; 80b Martin Thomas Photography/Alamy; 81 AA/M Chaplow; 82 Turespaña; 83 AA/M Chaplow; 84 Turespaña; 85 AA/R Strange; 86 AA/J Edmanson; 87 AA/M Chaplow; 88 AA/M Chaplow; 89 AA/R Strange; 90 AA/M Jourdan; 91 AA/M Jourdan; 92 AA/M Jourdan; 93 AA/M Jourdan; 94 Real Academia de Bellas Artes des San Fernando; 95 Alex Segre/Alamy; 96 Melba Photo Agency/Alamy; 96/97 Real Academia de Bellas Artes des San Fernando; 97 Real Academia de Bellas Artes des San Fernando; 98 Mooch Photography/Alamy;. 98/99 Mooch Photography/Alamy; 100 AA/M Jourdan; 101 AA/M Chaplow; 102(i) AA/M Chaplow; 102(ii) AA/M Chaplow; 102(iii) AA/M Jourdan; 102(iv) Centro de Tourismo de Madrid; 102(v) Centro de Tourismo de Madrid; 104t AA/M Chaplow; 104b Kevin Foy/Alamy; 105 AA/M Chaplow'; 106 AA/R Strange; 107 Alberto Paredes/Alamy; 108/109 AA/M Jourdan; 109 AA/M Jourdan; 110t Museo Nacional del Prado; 110b AA/M Jourdan; 112t Centro de Tourismo de Madrid; 112b AA/M Jourdan; 113 AA/M Jourdan; 114 AA/M Chaplow; 114/115 Centro de Tourismo de Madrid; 116/117 Centro de Tourismo de Madrid; 117 AA/R Strange; 118 StockImages/Alamy; 119 Centro de Tourismo de Madrid; 120/121 Centro de Tourismo de Madrid; 122 AA/M Chaplow; 123 AA/M Jourdan; 124 Turespaña; 125 AA/M Chaplow; 126(i) Turespaña; 126(ii) AA/M Chaplow; 126(iii) Alberto Paredes/Alamy; 126(iv) AA/R Strange; 126(v) dk/Alamy; 128 AA/R Strange; 130 Turespaña; 131 Turespaña; 133 Alberto Paredes/Alamy; 134 Museo Lazaro Galdiano; 135 Museo Lazaro Galdiano; 136 Museo Lazaro Galdiano; 137 Museo Lazaro Galdiano; 138 AA/M Chaplow; 139 AA/M Chaplow; 140 AA/M Chaplow; 141 AA/R Strange; 142t AA/R Strange; 142b AA/R Strange; 143 dk/Alamy; 144 Turespaña; 145 AA/R Strange; 146 AA/M Jourdan; 147 AA/M Chaplow; 148 AA/C Sawyer; 149 Lynne Evans/Alamy; 150 Turespaña; 151 Photodisc; 153 AA/M Jourdan; 154 AA/M Jourdan; 155 AA/M Jourdan; 156 Centro de Tourismo de Madrid; 157 AA/M Chaplow; 158 AA/M Chaplow; 159 Parque Warner Bros; 160 Centro de Tourismo de Madrid; 161 AA/M Chaplow; 162 AA/C Sawyer; 166 Centro de Tourismo de Madrid; 172 AA/C Sawyer; 178 ???; 182 AA/M Jourdan; 183 AA/M Chaplow; 187 AA/M Chaplow; 188 AA/M Chaplow

Every effort has been made to trace the copyright holders, and we apologise in advance for any accidental errors. We would be happy to apply the corrections in the following edition of this publication.

The Automobile Association would like to thank all other contributors to this publication.